CLASSICS OF ASIAN AMERICAN LITERATURE

AWAKE IN THE RIVER

&

SHEDDING SILENCE

JANICE MIRIKITANI

FOREWORD BY
JULIANA CHANG

UNIVERSITY OF WASHINGTON PRESS

Seattle

Awake in the River and Shedding Silence was made possible in part by a grant from the Shawn Wong Book Fund, which supports the publication of books on Asian American history and culture. Shawn Wong would also like to thank and acknowledge the generous additional support for this publication from Mary in Rome.

Design by Doug Goewey
Composed in Scala OT, typeface designed by Martin Majoor

26   25   24   23   22   5   4   3   2   1

Printed and bound in the United States of America

UNIVERSITY OF WASHINGTON PRESS
uwapress.uw.edu

LIBRARY OF CONGRESS CATALOGING-IN-PUBLICATION DATA
Names: Mirikitani, Janice, author.
Title: Awake in the river and Shedding silence / Janice Mirikitani.
Description: Seattle : University of Washington Press, [2021] | Series: Classics of Asian American literature | Includes bibliographical references.
Identifiers: LCCN 2021034570 (print) | LCCN 2021034571 (ebook) | ISBN 9780295749570 (hardcover) | ISBN 9780295749587 (paperback) | ISBN 9780295749594 (ebook)
Subjects: LCGFT: Poetry.
Classification: LCC PS3563.I696 A93 2021 (print) | LCC PS3563.I696 (ebook) | DDC 811/.54—dc23
LC record available at https://lccn.loc.gov/2021034570
LC ebook record available at https://lccn.loc.gov/2021034571

♾ This paper meets the requirements of ANSI/NISO Z39.48-1992 (Permanence of Paper).

CONTENTS

SHEDDING SILENCE

Without Tongue

It Isn't Easy

FOREWORD

Juliana Chang

I was seventeen when I first saw Janice Mirikitani take the stage at Zeller-bach Auditorium. I was a first-year student at the University of California, Berkeley, and the anti-apartheid movement had galvanized the campus in the spring of 1985. I attended nightly meetings during the occupation of Sproul Plaza, learning from activists how to analyze and resist systemic racism—global and local.

Mirikitani was one of the featured speakers at a women of color poetry reading. In my memory, she was resplendent in a shimmery ensemble, gloriously made up in red lipstick and dark eyeliner, haloed with a mane of black wavy hair, fierce and riveting in her delivery.

I loved poetry and had compulsively checked out books by Anne Sexton and Adrienne Rich from my high school library. I had never heard of an Asian American poet before.

I still remember my exuberance. An Asian American woman poet! Reading in solidarity with women of color across the globe. The shock waves reverberated and became part of the vibration of my everyday life. I sought out courses in women's studies and ethnic studies. I combed through the Asian American studies library and pored over publications from the Asian American movement of the 1970s, many of which featured the writings of Mirikitani: *Counterpoint, Asian-American Heritage, Bridge*. I discovered that Mirikitani was a key architect of early Asian American and Third World cultural politics, having edited and co-edited founding publications of this era: *Aion* (1970–71), *Third World Women* (1972), *Time to Greez! Incantations from the Third World* (1975). As the '70s turned into the '80s, she continued her collaborative editorial work with *Ayumi: A Japanese American Anthology* (1981) and *Making Waves: An Anthology of Writings by and about Asian American Women* (1989). During this period, Mirikitani also took on major leadership roles at Glide Memorial Church and the Glide Foundation, which provided social services and did advocacy work for marginalized communities in San Francisco.

The term "Asian American," which provided a conceptual category for the literature I was discovering, was coined and popularized in 1968 by student activists as a pan-ethnic formation. Timothy Yu argues that the genre of poetry, abundantly featured in many early publications, was "central" and "vital to the Asian American political project." He considers Asian American poetry of this period an avant-garde formation, "a grouping that defined itself not just through race, but through bold experiments with form and style in the search for an Asian American aesthetic."[1]

Critics and scholars have posited *Aiiieeeee! An Anthology of Asian American Writers* (1974) as foundational to the fields of Asian American literature and culture. The curatorial work of its editors helped to highlight and recover important mid-twentieth-century Chinese, Japanese, and Filipino American writers. Meanwhile, its introduction fired off a fusillade of shots against white supremacy and anti-Asian racism, even as it also elicited criticism for disparaging Asian American writers who did not seem sufficiently authentic, many of whom were women.

I believe we should situate Mirikitani's editorial and creative work along the same continuum as that of the editors of *Aiiieeeee!* Her assemblages, archetypes, tropes, and cadences, like theirs, brought new and subversive Asian American cultures and sensibilities into being. But poetry, though vital to independently published 1970s movement publications, became less widely circulated than prose fiction and nonfiction as corporate publishers sought to capitalize on multiculturalism in the '80s and '90s. And while masculine rage against white supremacy as articulated in the introduction to *Aiiieeeee!* is comprehended as political, defiant writing by women of color can be treated less as representative of a group and more as contained within categories like "individual" or "emotional." For these reasons, Mirikitani's status as also foundational to Asian American literary and cultural studies has not been as conspicuous as it could or should be. Mirikitani's work deserves greater recognition for its formative role not only in fashioning early Asian American cultural and political sensibilities but also in marking them from the beginning as what we would now call intersectional as well as coalitional. Gender and race are inextricable in her poems, and Asian American politics are intentionally articulated with the liberation of other people of color in the United States and around the world.

From the vantage point of the early twenty-first century, we can see how Mirikitani's creative and community work were visionary and prophetic, creating new collectives and new cultural politics. They laid the groundwork for much of today's paradigms and discourses: #StopAsianHate, women of color feminisms, #MeToo, decolonization, Black Lives Matter, race and mental health. The populist tenor of her writing was a precursor to the spoken word movement that blossomed in the 1990s and 2000s, and to poetry shared on social media—poems that could be comprehended in a flash, on the go, in interstitial moments. Literary magazines like *Aion*, widely acknowledged as the first pan-ethnic Asian American literary magazine, helped pave the way for current Asian American and Pacific Islander literary and poetry journals like *Kartika Review* and *Lantern Review*.

Mirikitani was an early artist of women of color feminisms. The perspectives of Asian American women and girls are frequently centered in her poems, and pieces like "Spoils of War," "Recipe," "Doreen," and "Slaying Dragon Ladies" depict and protest the devaluation and violation of Asian American women and girls. One of her poetic strategies is to incorporate the voices of dominant ideology in her poems, to illustrate how racial violence at macro and micro levels is put into practice and internalized by women of color. "Recipe," taking on the imperative voice of the cookbook genre, consists entirely of instructions for modifying Asian eye shape. Its last command, "Do not cry," explicitly suppresses and implicitly acknowledges the sorrow engendered by this message that one's eyes are unacceptable as they are.

Just as Mirikitani's racial analysis always included gender, so too her gendered analysis always included race. When a white woman in the poem "Ms." takes offense at being addressed as "miss," the speaker deflates the righteousness of white liberal feminism and observes that her privileged position as a white woman derives from indigenous dispossession, racialized labor, and imperialist violence.

> sheltered as you are by mansions
>   built on Indian land
>
> your diamonds shipped with slaves from Africa
> your underwear washed by Chinese laundries
> your house cleaned by my grandmother
> . . . .
> And when you quit
> killing us
> for democracy
> and stop calling ME *gook*

I will call you
Whatever you like.

Mirikitani was ahead of her time in being outspoken about the impact
of race and gender on mental health, including psychosomatic damage
engendered by state, sexual, and family violence and trauma. "Crazy
Alice" paints a portrait of a woman driven mad by the incarceration of
Japanese Americans during World War II. Aunt Alice's relatives laugh
at her "tattered coat" and confusion of family names. The speaker, how-
ever, respects Alice's unflinching acknowledgment of having "touched
the sun," of being scalded by the brutal forces of imprisonment, intimate
partner violence, and sexual exploitation.

While the model minority myth emerging in the 1960s seems a more
benign racial formation than the 1940s depiction of Japanese Americans
as "enemy aliens," it can have fatal consequences, as indexed by high rates
of suicide among Asian American students, particularly Asian American
women. "Suicide Note" speaks in the voice of a student apologizing to her
parents for *"having received less than a perfect four point grade average."* The
student is figured as a bird whose wings are crippled by a litany of debilitat-
ing messages. "Not good enough," "not smart enough," "not pretty enough"
are repeated like a chant or mantra. The lack of noun or verb indicates
the erasure of subjectivity and agency; only measurements are forcefully
asserted. The inhospitable environment of family, school, and society is fig-
ured by the shards of ice that wound the bird and the snow that buries her.

In a culture that blamed women and girls for sexual assault and abuse,
Mirikitani's poems dared to speak up about rape, molestation, and incest
from the perspective of the survivor. In "Zipper," the titular image figures
the forcible opening of the body's boundaries even as the subject's voice
remains contained and suppressed.

No silent prayer,
no whisper of disgrace,
no speechless pain
would keep the teeth
clenched. Zipper
undone.
A jagged sneer across her flesh.

While the first three line breaks occur more organically, at the end of
cohesive phrases where one could release or take a breath, the following

two line breaks feel more unnatural, causing one to hold one's breath in suspense. The release of breath at the conclusion, when one encounters the spikiness and cruelty ("jagged sneer") inflicted on the speaker, creates a sense of devastating finality. And the fact that the last two phrases consist of nouns, adjectives, and prepositional phrases but no verbs indexes the unspeakability of the acts that were committed.

In poems like "Lullabye," published in 1974, the daughter perceives her mother's silence about internment as life-depleting.[2] For this reason, the mother's subsequent testimony in 1980 before the Commission on Wartime Relocation and Internment of Civilians is presented in "Breaking Silence" as a watershed, a "miracle" of "lightning and justice." So powerfully was this moment rendered in the poem that its title was selected to also name a major anthology of Asian American poetry published by Greenfield Review Press in 1983.[3]

Thanks to writers like Mirikitani, breaking silence has become a commonplace maxim for Asian American activism. Literary critics have complicated the association of silence with absence or passivity, investigating the nuances of apparent speechlessness in books such as *Articulate Silences* and *Tell This Silence*. It can be easy to take this trope for granted, but we should remember why it is so transformative. For Mirikitani, politics and mental health are intertwined. People who are rendered deviant through race and gendered formations are shamed for their differences and stigmatized for speaking up. Breaking silence refuses the discipline and punishment of racialized, gendered shame. Genres like poetry and narrative give shape to the disarray and turmoil of racial and sexual trauma. In creating meaning from such experiences, creative and expressive writing can be practices of healing.

Because of their provocative, cathartic, and therapeutic qualities, the pieces in Mirikitani's oeuvre that have garnered the most attention are those that protest injustice. But a poem like "A Lecherous Poem to Toshiro Mifune" also paved the way for claiming a politics of pleasure and joy for women of color.

> i am
> that hair tearing
> hara-kiri prone/
> longing/licking
> body-burning-for-you
> woman of the dunes.

Proclaiming erotic desire, the speaker does not refuse shame so much as transform it into a charged sense of vitality and carnality. "Drowning in the Yellow River" indicts the microaggressions of white male suitors, but the adolescent speaker cheekily rhymes jazz lingo and Japanese ("stop suckin' on my neck daddy-o/gotta go/to the obenjo") and audaciously produces a "pee-drowned scarf," asserting her embodied yellowness while making out with "white boys." And let's not overlook the taboo pleasures of revenge for women of color, as in "Slaying Dragon Ladies." The dragon lady is a racialized fantasy of exotic oriental villainy, her evil-doings senseless and depraved. Mirikitani reclaims meaning and redemption for the dragon lady's power by figuring her as a writer-avenger.

> My hands are steady.
> Pentipped fingers
> drenched in ink.
> Ready for the slaying.

> You will know me.

Like many artists of the Third Worldist movement of the 1970s in the Bay Area, Mirikitani explicitly protests US militarism and imperialism in poems like "Loving from Vietnam to Zimbabwe," "A Certain Kind of Madness," "Jungle Rot and Open Arms," and "Assaults and Invasions." But her critique of Western imperialism can be found not only in content but also in form. In her poetics, she refuses and offers alternatives to the abstraction, individualism, and rationalism of Western, colonial paradigms of poetry and culture.

Against abstract universalism, her poems are particular and embodied. Against the individual lyric "I," her poems are archetypal and channel multitudes. Consider the abundance of poems addressing grandparents, parents, aunts and uncles, lovers and partners, children, multiple generations: "For My Father," "Sing with Your Body," "Desert Flowers," "The First Generation," "The Fisherman," "In Remembrance," "Breaking Tradition," "A Song for You." Against rationalism, her poems are incantations, casting spells that conjure visions, unbury voices, and empower the vulnerable.

"We, the Dangerous" begins with a litany of oaths, creating an atmosphere of liturgy and ceremony.

> I swore
> it would not devour me

I swore
it would not humble me
I swore
it would not break me.

The poem then alternates between stanzas of "they" and "we." "They" issue commands for incarceration, labor exploitation, and the commitment of wartime atrocities. "We" voices a collective that is associated with nature and earth, therefore deemed exploitable and disposable.

And they commanded we dwell in the desert
Our children be spawn of barbed wire and barracks

We, closer to the earth
. . . .

And they would have us make the garden
Rake the grass to soothe their feet

We, akin to the jungle,
. . . .

And they would have us skin their fish
. . . .

We, who awake in the river
. . . .

And they would have us strange scented women,
Round shouldered/strong and yellow/like the moon
to pull the thread to the cloth
to loosen their backs massaged in myth

We, who fill the secret bed,
. . . .

And they would dress us in napalm,
Skin shred to clothe the earth,
Bodies filling pock marked fields.

Mirikitani's writing is profoundly elemental. Water, fire, metal, earth, and air manifest in her oeuvre as rivers, the sun, blades, the desert, and breath. Plants, animals, and human body parts are similarly strewed across her poems and stories. This is what gives her writing a sense of primal power. We see these kinds of elemental figures in "We, the Dangerous": the metal of barbed wire, the wood of barracks, the fire of napalm, grass and garden, the moon. While the collective "we" is presumably made subordinate by being deemed "closer to the earth," Mirikitani reclaims this elemental status and gives the "we" the power of mythology.

Note the comma, however, in the title "We, the Dangerous." The "We" is not an already established grouping. It is the naming of the coalition, the feeling of the "we" that then imbues the collective with power. In this way, Mirikitani weds politics with mythology, which she also does in the poem's conclusion, merging the elemental and the historical.

> We, the dangerous,
> Dwelling in the ocean.
> Akin to the jungle.
> Close to the earth.
>
> Hiroshima
> Vietnam
> Tule Lake
>
> And yet we were not devoured
> And yet we were not humbled
> And yet we are not broken.

The first two lines of the last stanza invoke a history of resistance, and the final line switches from past to present tense, making stalwart the "we" that continues. The present tense allows for a reading of the poem as not just a text of its compositional era but one that resonates into the future, into the present of the reader. With its anaphoric repetition, "We, the Dangerous" enacts poetry as incantation, a ceremony of survival, a spell to ward off evil.

Mirikitani's poetry and poetics fortify her readers, ensuring we are ready for the fight. This assemblage is a call, a manifesto, a brief, an accusation, an interrogation. And more. Her poems call forth the dead and the nonhuman: familial ancestors, fallen comrades, owls with open mouths, tortoise eggs ready to hatch. In her world, these are not "others." Meet and greet them as you read this collection, as you join forces with her circle of "we."

NOTES

1   Timothy Yu, *Race and the Avant-Garde: Experimental and Asian American Poetry Since 1965* (Stanford: Stanford University Press, 2009), 74, 73.

2   "Lullabye" was published in the anthology *Asian-American Heritage* and subsequently included in *Awake in the River*. David Hsin-Fu Wand, ed., *Asian-American Heritage: An Anthology of Prose and Poetry* (New York: Washington Square Press, 1974).

3   Joseph Bruchac, ed., *Breaking Silence: An Anthology of Contemporary Asian American Poets* (New York: The Greenfield Review Press, 1983).

AWAKE IN THE RIVER
&
SHEDDING SILENCE

AWAKE IN THE RIVER

. . . .
And yet,
      we were not devoured
      we were not humbled
      we are not broken.

FOR MY FATHER

He came over the ocean
carrying Mt. Fuji
on his back/Tule Lake on his chest
hacked through the brush
of deserts
and made them grow
strawberries

      we stole berries
      from the stem
      we could not afford them
      for breakfast

his eyes held
nothing
as he whipped us
for stealing.

the desert had dried
his soul.

wordless
he sold
the rich,
full berries
to hakujines
whose children
pointed at our eyes

      they ate fresh
      strawberries
      with cream.

Father,
I wanted to scream
at your silence.
Your strength
was a stranger
I could never touch.

      iron
      in your eyes
      to shield
      the pain
      to shield desert-like wind
      from patches
      of strawberries
      grown
      from
      tears.

SING WITH YOUR BODY

for my daughter, Tianne Tsukiko

We love with great difficulty
spinning in one place
afraid to create
        spaces
             new rhythm

the beat of a child
dangled by her own inner ear
takes Aretha with her

            upstairs,   somewhere
go quickly, Tskuiko,

            into your circled dance
go quickly

            before your steps are
            halted by who you are not

go quickly

            to learn the mixed
            sounds of your tongue,

go quickly

            to who you are

            before

                your mother swallows
                what she has lost.

AUGUST 6

Yesterday
a thousand cranes
were flying.
Hiroshima,
your children
still dying
                    and they said

                    it saved many lives

the great white heat
that shook flesh from bone
melted bone
to dust
                    and they said
                    it was merciful

yesterday
a thousand cranes
were flying.
Obachan
offered omame
to her radiant Buddha
incense smoking miniature
mushrooms
her lips moving
in prayer
for sister they found
tattooed to the ground
a fleshless shadow on Hiroshima soil

                    and they said
                    Nagasaki

Yesterday
a woman
bore a child
with fingers
growing from her neck
shoulder
empty

       and they said
       the arms race

Today
a thousand cranes
are flying
and in expensive waiting rooms
of Hiroshima, California
are blood counts
sucked by the white death

       and they said
       it might happen again

tonight
while
everyone sleeps
memoryless
the night wind
flutters like a thousand wings
how many ears will hear
the whisper
"Hiroshima"
from a child's
armless shoulder
puckered
like a kiss?

LOVING FROM VIETNAM TO ZIMBABWE

Here in this crimson
room
with silk skimming our skin
I shape into thought
these strange burnings
starting in my fingertips
as they lick your nipples,
hairs standing to the touch.

       You are marching in
       the delta
       the river water
       at your boots
       sucking through the leather
       sand has caked your color yellow.

Your chest moves
to the rhythm of my heart
warm skin singing

       you plod weighted by
       days of marching
       nights of terror
       holding this patch of ground
       shaped like a crotch.

my teeth on your
shoulder
hungry to enter your flesh
as you call me strange names.

       water/water
       sinking sand
       they are coming
       as you raise the blade
       of your bayonet
       clean it with
       your sweat.

My mouth driven
to your thighs
the sweet inside
just below the swinging
songs of your life.

> Deeper into
> the mekong
> the grass has eyes
> the wind has flesh
> and you feel the trigger
> pressed back for release

your thighs tremble
your long fingers like marsh grass
in my hair
as i reach down
onto Mt. Inyangani

> you have seen them
> hanging in the trees
> after american troops
> had finished/
> slanted eyes bugging
> crooked necks
> genitals swinging from
> their mouths.

Sweat from your neck
I think they are tears
as i move
into the grassy plain
of your chest.

> You never saw them
> but knew they looked like me
> and you got sick a lot
> wondering what color
> their blood.

As I hold
your skin between my
teeth
I can feel the blood
pulsing
on my tongue
spurting like the
beginning of
Zambezi   River.

                You turned in your rage
                knowing how they have used you.
                Not the invisible ones
                whose soil you were sent to seize
                but those behind you
            .   pushing you
                pulling
                pulling
                your trigger.

And I massage
your back
large/black like the shadowed
belly of a leaf
as you in
your stillness
hold me like
a bird.

                they stripped you
                held you down
                in the sand
                took the bayonet off your gun
                and began to slice
                lopped off your head
                and expected you to die.

I, in the
heavy hot air
between us,
in the crimson room
that begins to blur
feel you enter
my harbor/kiss the lips
of my soul
Call me Strange Names

        hanoi
        bachmai
        haiphong

loving in this world
is the sliver splinting
edge
is the dare
in the teeth of the tiger
the pain of jungle rot
the horror of flesh unsealed
the danger of surviving.

DESERT FLOWERS

Flowers
faded
in the desert wind.
No flowers grow
where dust winds blow
and rain is like
a dry heave moan.

Mama, did you dream about that
beau who would take you
away from it all,
who would show you
in his '41 ford
and tell you how soft
your hands
like the silk kimono
you folded for the wedding?
Make you forget
about That place,
the back bending
wind that fell like a wall,
drowned all your geraniums
and flooded the shed
where you tried to sleep
away hyenas?
And mama,
bending in the candlelight,
after lights out in barracks,
an ageless shadow
grows victory flowers
made from crepe paper,
shaping those petals
like the tears
your eyes bled.
Your fingers
knotted at knuckles
wounded, winding around wire stems
the tiny, sloganed banner:

"america for americans."

Did you dream
of the shiny ford
(only always a dream)
ride your youth
like the wind
in the headless night?

Flowers
2¢ a dozen,
flowers for American Legions
worn like a badge
on america's lapel
made in post-concentration camps
by candlelight.
Flowers
watered
by the spit
of "no japs wanted here,"
planted in poverty
of postwar relocations,
plucked by
victory's veterans.

Mama, do you dream
of the wall of wind
that falls
on your limbless desert,
on stems
brimming with petals/crushed
crepe paper
growing
from the crippled
mouth of your hand?

Your tears, mama,
have nourished us.
Your children
like pollen
scatter in the wind.

WATERGATE, U.S.

The deadliest evil is when "recognized"
power works against the good of all people . . .
                                        Cecil Williams

It is a time like no other.
        In the streets
        the children
        play with dogs
        who have smelled
        the danger of sleepless giants
        frightened and dying
        fucking their bitches
        in fantasies of
        young men.

The heat is unbearable.
Dried, white heat
sweating with peoples' hunger

It is a time like no other

        The dried, white dying giants
        walk their women
        who suck the erect heat
        of air
        led by the leash of unfulfilled
        promises
        splaying their smell
        for hot, young men
        held hungry,
        hopeless.

It is a time like no other

    the woman
    dangled like meat
    on a spear
    by dried white dying giants
    who lie about their love for women
    their hate for themselves.

It is a time like no other

    When cannibals
    and giants
    battle
    for the smell of the woman
    and the giants' limbs
    torn, rent
    leaving only his member
    dangled on a spear.

The woman eats it

    gags
    gives up her mind
    clothes her body
    with her smell
    for bait
    while the hot
    young men
    wait
    hopeful
    hungry
to become giants.

THE FIRST GENERATION

Elegy to my grandmother

Bent and knotted as a wintered vine
she watched her daughters grow from her
in a hybrid land
and the grandchildren thick around
no longer her own.

> Hototogisu naki naki
> *(The cuckoo cries cries*

She grew wisteria
as a temple
in her garden
and there kept her private peace

> Oto hitori ame de ato
> *the only sound after rain*

The children mocked the old ways
shook the fragile vines in their play
while silently she made a wreath
of the dying blossoms

> shizuka no jimen arau
> *washes the land with quiet)*

Her love wore long
as my sorrow.
The withered roots
have given back beauty to the soil.

JAPS

(Inspired by a play by Hiroshi Kashiwagi
Plums Can Wait *about migrant Japanese*
American farmers after WWII)

Owls with open mouths
watch mutely
as rapists come
and ravage the plums
hanging heavy
like a waiting woman's breast.
They will soften
before the boxes are built.
The slant eyed midget
works harder
sweats more
as the boss's wife
watches from her shaded window
the short arms
lugging long planks,
nails
protruding from his palms.
She wanted to hate him, who
never spoke
planeing the wood
nailing them tightly together
like thighs.
Owls with open mouths
watch
as the rapists
lurk behind
shaded windows
wondering at midgets
quickening among the plums,
moving faster
strides shorter,
and the plums
like ripe breasts
always above his reach.

She felt
rage at the slant eyed
short armed
quick moving
midget/the jap
who made her
watch the walls at night
when sleepless
the owls called.
The boss would not
let him go
he worked too well.
And the wife
chipping the midget
like a knife,
her words/hate
as she tried to make
him/weaker/anything
and he would
bend/silently/packing boxes
with full/soft plums.
Owls with open mouths
see the rapist
offer the midget
a 5¢ raise in pay/a day
if he will fuck
the wife.
The midget jap
pins the long planks
with nails
from his hands
making boxes
as the wife rapist
lurks behind the window shade
while flies collide
over the dead owl,
eyes staring
haunts her.

if you're too dark
they will kill you.
if you're too swift
they will cripple you.
if you're too strong
they will buy you.
if you're too beautiful
they will rape you.

Watch with eyes open
speak darkly
turn your head like the owl
behind you.
They are coming
to nail you to boxes.

A CERTAIN KIND OF MADNESS

After the assassination of
Orlando Letelier of Chile &
Steve Biko of South Africa

Incense
white paper
Somber kimono sleeves
lapping at the coffin.
Water spilling
from each face,
burying auntie.
My mother is there
trying to hide me.
The smell of dead bodies
makes my mind
pain.
It's my form of madness.

After the war,
auntie would cry
at night
tried to bury her face in the mattress
so we wouldn't hear.
And they would whisper
about her forgetfulness
her thinness
and trembling that would not stop.
In frozen silence
the black shoes gather
at the incense cup.
Momma, you wonder why I don't speak
anymore.
The smell of dead bodies
makes my mind pain
It's my form of madness

When we saw Letelier blown up
in a car, front screen
you said he must've done something bad.

I told you
there are hunters who kill by color:

    the gold tinted flesh
    that shines in its sweat
    rice eating creatures
    who plant in the sea.
    brown backed bodies
    blended to earth
    that once ran free
    in mountains behind Managua.
    black glistening
    shoulders moving to
    wind sobs, in the
    streets of Soweto.

There are those
who are hunted and killed for pleasure.

    When Biko went
    they thought silence would
    follow
    like rows of white stones.

What form of madness?

Did auntie
eat the sandwich
left on the road for ants?
You said
hunger is not a question
it is a disgrace.
Don't speak of it.

You are mad, you said
when I asked you
about the train
we boarded years ago
for those cages in the desert.
Didn't you know
they were smiling/smiling
while you
thrashed like a rabbit
entangled in barbed wire.

Momma, did we do something bad?

There are hunters who kill beauty
for pleasure
to fill their coffers
from the sale of your flesh
who kill free moving things
to stop them from hurting their eyes.

The smell of dead bodies
It's my form of madness.
But I tell you

        These words I do speak
        I don't do well in a cage.
        It's lonely there.
        I won't dwell in a cage
        It's my form of madness.

JUNGLE ROT AND OPEN ARMS

for a Vietnam Veteran brother, ex-prisoner

Leavenworth
and jungle rot
brought him
back to us
brimming with hate
and disbelief
in love or
sympathy.

his johnnywalker red
eyes
tore at my words
shred my flesh
made naked my
emptiness.

my anger
for the enemy heads
of state
boiled to nothing
        nothing
in the wake
of his rage

jungle rot
had sucked his bones,
his skin fell
like the monsoon
his brain
in a cast in Leavenworth.

In the midst
of genocide
he fell in love
in Vietnam.

"Her hair was
long and dark—like yours"
        he said
"her eyes held the
sixth moon
and when she smiled
the sky opened
and I fell through.

I would crawl
in the tall grasses
to her village

and sleep the war
away with her
like a child on my thighs

I did not know
of the raid

and woke

with her arm
still clasping mine

I could not find
the rest of her

so I buried her arm
and marked my grave."

We sat in a silence
that mocks fools
that lifts us to the final language.

his breath sapped by B-52's
his eyes blinded by the blood of children
his hands bound to bayonets
his soul buried in a shallow grave

i stood amidst
his wreckage
and wept for myself.

so where is my
political education? my
rhetoric answers to everything? my
theory into practice? my
intensification of life in art?

words
are
like
the stone,
the gravemarker
over an arm
in Vietnam.

SALAD

The woman
did not mean to
offend me,

her blue eyes
blinking
at the glint
of my blade,

as I cut
precisely
like magic
the cucumber in
exact, even,
quick slices.

Do you orientals
do everything
so neatly?

MS.

I got into a thing
with someone
because I called her
miss ann/hearst/rockerfeller/hughes
instead of ms.

I said
it was a waste of time
worrying about it.

Her lips pressed white
thinning words like pins
pricking me—a victim of sexism.

I wanted to
call her what
she deserved
but knowing it would please her
instead
I said,

> white lace & satin was never soiled by
> > sexism
> sheltered as you are by mansions
> > built on Indian land
>
> your diamonds shipped with slaves from Africa
> your underwear washed by Chinese laundries
> your house cleaned by my grandmother

so do not push me any further.

And when you quit
killing us
for democracy
and stop calling ME *gook*.

I will call you
whatever you like.

I HATE YOU
WOMAN

YOU IN YOUR SMALL MIND
SQUEEZING INSECURITIES
GRAPPLING AFTER GOSSIP MINDED
BOURGEOIS BIGOTS

I HATE YOU
WOMAN

YOUR FUMBLING MISINTERPRETATIONS
CONTROLLING LIVES
THAT ARE NOT YOURS
BECAUSE YOU CANNOT LIVE FOR YOURSELF

I HATE YOU
WOMAN

YOUR MANIPULATION
GUILT CREATING—PUTTING INTO BOXES
EVERYTHING YOU DON'T WANT TO
UNDERSTAND. DON'T GIVE ME THIS SHIT.

I HATE YOU
WOMAN

BECAUSE YOU CANNOT
KEEP YOUR MAN
YOU ONLY CAN NAG HIM
INTO SUBMISSION

I HATE YOU
WOMAN

FOR IMPOSING YOUR LIFE
IN MINE
FOR STEALING MY ENERGY
AND TIME
FOR BEING IN MY MIND

I HATE YOU
WOMAN

FOR YOUR LIES
TO YOURSELF
FOR THE SMALL CAUSES
YOU UNDERTAKE TO
LIMIT YOUR EGO

I HATE YOU
WOMAN

FOR YOUR COLD
MISCOMPREHENSION
YOUR SELF PITY
AND DECEPTION
YOUR MINDLESS CONTRACEPTION
AGAINST LIFE

I HATE YOU
WOMAN

YOU

WHO ARE

MIRRORED

IN ME.

BITCHES DON'T WAIT

Stayed up
half the night
wondering
knowing
where are you
it's better
to have
more than one
it makes you
anxious to come back
to me when you're thru.
Bitches don't wait,
don't play those games
sleeping around
with fools
who don't care
about my fine
sensitive woman nature.
i'd rather
stand on the corner
in my short
slit chong sam
or my wide necked
kimono
massaging
muscles for a dime
in some anonymous
room
warm, moist,
and smelling like
that opening
from where we all come
the room
like a wide screaming
mouth
melting coconut oil
on you

after a steaming bath
your bodies dripping
like my eyes
we won't get bored
'cause i won't even know you.

my virginal soul
will wait
and wait
for you.
keeping the bed
like an altar
wrap the sheets
on your feet
finger your hem
and you will always
return.
Does it hurt
because i know you are
with the one you're with
and you do your love thing
as i wait here
not present to you?
It hurts
'cause i would
rather write a better line
stroke poems
like antelope
feel the Miles
blues like warm
honey
capture tigers
in China
and sleep in the folds
of their great breathing shanks.
i will go now to my street
when the work is done
coat my skin
with a violet gown
haloed with hood

oils in my hands
water
in my vessel
a net in
my thighs
and i will
sell
my body for a dime

        while i don't wait
        for you.

NAKAMA

to comrade sisters
before me, beyond me.

The cherry blossoms
are bursting

female swans
calling
on the lake
beckoning with dark beaks

This time
the day spilling like bright flowers
I thought of you
sisters

    ebony bones
    building empires
    empowering brothers
    the dark wombs
    spilling with the future

mujer
nakama

    browned in sun work
    blessing the earth with boundless beauty
    pounding the rice
    dancing the dance
        that makes our brothers rise.

my child
is singing to herself
and she is
growing
she is woman
shining
as she tends her flowers, asks me

why do they die?

why do they always die?

my child
i want to enclose you
and tell you about the
cherry

the blossoms do not die
they are
eternal in beauty
bursting like red suns
when it is time

And when it is time
they ascend
in the wind to some new place
carrying their
sweet scent
unwithered
they remain
everlasting
like the strain
of songs
of poems
of our sisters
   our brothers

why do they die?

why do they die?

They do not die
my child

like you
shining
woman
reflecting
my love

carrying me
in you
carrying the time

like the beautiful cherry
bursting like suns

we do not die

THE WINNER

Aunt Sumi was a shadow with poorly fitted teeth. I remember her smile because the rest of her face was hidden by long surviving bruises.

> Tets would come home
> yell about the Chinamen
> who hung around the shed
> out back, playing ma jong
> after they had done their work.

Sumi cringed around corners, listening to a little joy, snatching the virile movement of arms swinging down tiles.

After her illness, I was sent to help clean her house. She seemed unable to organize herself, not knowing what to do next. The dishes would begin to smell from 3 day fish and hamu, still sticking on the tin.

She never heard me as I complained about the hard work made harder by her neglect. She would smile and tell me how much I had grown since the last time she had seen me, a week ago.

> O, the men
> will be after you
> soon enough.
> You can have your pick
> if you're careful.
> Perfect/You've got to be
> perfect.

Her words bleeding off my back, as I dusted and swept.

> He used to be a good man
> bring me flowers
> Take me
> to the races
> and show me
> a fine time
> Let me bet
> a couple of dollars
> on the high stepping one
> with a white star

on her head
And I would wear
my dress with the roses on it
and my white shoes
And he would laugh a lot
when I jumped up and down
screaming the Star in
on a win.

She knew the two worlds well. Being what she dreamed. Dreaming
what she was not. She would tell me to be restrained. To be refined and
dignified. Not to talk a lot and say the wrong things. Not to to smile too
much. Only in silence will men imagine perfection.

But Tets
would tell me he loved
my teeth.
They were white and well shaped
and they lit up my face when
I talked.

And she told me to be good. In everything. If you're graceful they will
woo you forever. If you are quiet, they will want to marry you. If you are
obedient, you will remind them of their mother. You must never show
them that you are smart. Or that you long for anything else except the
world they can give you.

Star knew she was
the best.
Her lovely head high
at the starting gate,
her step sassy with pride
When she ran
my breath would stop.
She was so free.
And she was a winner
I could tell.
The jockey would never have
to use the whip on her.
I told Tets
they never whip a winner.

I would stop and look at Sumi's face. It was almost beautiful in the light, talking about Tets back then, her love for the courage of that horse. Her skin translucent through the bruises. Her eyes took on a shine that was not in this world. Her forehead was smooth with happiness and her lips were full, spilling those memories.

Outside we could hear the men laughing. Someone had won. Looey and his friends from other farms. Looey spoke little English when he came to this country. Tets and Sumi took him in. Tets did not like him at all.

> Chinamen
> all alike
> rather gamble
> and sleep
> than work.

Looey was a practical solution to their hardships when they returned from the camps. The farm did not yield enough for profit, and Looey was free labor in exchange for a place to stay. Tets took on work other places, fixing cars and doing carpentry for hakujines.

I don't know when the beatings began. I overheard momma say that after the war, when times were so bad, Tets would get drunk a lot and stay away. Sumi, who could never keep her mouth shut, would nag him, and she'd come over wearing dark glasses because her eyes were so swollen and black. It was like that for years.

Dusting the glass cases that held fine dolls from Japan, one dressed in a purple kimono with gold woven onto the obi, with white cranes embroidered on its sleeve, face porcelained white, Sumi would follow my movements, jumping in time.

> The doll from Japan
> his mother sent
> before the war
> We gave it to the Johanssens
> to keep for us
> when we went into camp,
> and Tets into the army.
> I was so proud
> of him in uniform.
> He was handsome
> And before he left
> he was very kind to me.

Her eyes wandered far. I wondered if she was silent in their lovemaking.
She merged time.

> Tets and I
> once
> when love flowed,
> we, in stride as one.
> It was a feeling
> like watching Star
> run
> against the wind
> muscles rubbing
> other horses
> as she passed
> her neck stretching
> to make her legs
> reach farther
> And for a moment
> with all flesh straining
> with nostrils
> enlarging to suck more breath
> I thought my heart would burst.

Breaking the memory, she moved to the kitchen. Too young . . . she
mumbled, started a task, stopped, began to wander again.

> The last time
> I saw him
> I thought I was finished.
> He used his fists
> broke a lot of dishes
> that doll too.
> Looey tried to stop him
> but he was bleeding
> and dazed.
> Tets had the strength
> of madness
> I blacked out, came to
> with him straddling me
> my dress wet
> his fists in my belly

I couldn't move
with him sitting on me like that
my mouth full
of teeth rattling
and my hair was
scattered around me on the floor.
I knew I was going to die
His eyes told me
His eyes, fixed, dark, foreign
while his arms
kept coming down
whipping the sides of my face.

Sumi had been in the hospital, not waking for three days. Tets had left, and we never saw him again. They kept her for weeks. Testing, probing, useless treatments. She was not the same.

She married Looey. He was gentle, patient with her illness, her toothless clucking. The family was upset for a long time. People were talking too much. Obachan's heart broke and Ojichan would not permit her name to be uttered in his house again. Momma said that Tets had come home and found Sumi and the Chinaman in bed.

Those were some days
Tets laughing
as I stood on the railing
near home stretch
That horse coming around the bend
like an army
my legs
pumping Star in
jumping for her freedom
from the other horses trying to
block her/capture her
as she sucked in the wind.
And me,
leaping to the finish line
screaming for the
winner.

LOOKING FOR A POEM

. . . What's Pablo up to? I'm here. If you
look for me in the street, you'll find me there
tuning my fiddle, ready to sing and to die . . .
                    Pablo Neruda

I wander
thru the rubble
of images cast aside

            rain, swelling from old wood,
            a house smelling of generations
            now asleep,
            fish in ancient dance for our birth,
            a broken hoe,
            pickled vegetables,
            fire of war/empty eyes/
            charred bones.

The poem
lies here somewhere
as easy as a human kiss
but when I'm asked
why not a love poem,
anger is easier.
Frantic,
I search until too tired.
Retreat to his words
and he shouts:

    "Look for me in the street(s).
        You'll find me there . . . ready to sing or to die . . ."

Epigraph quoted from "For Everybody," by Pablo Neruda, *Five Decades: Poems 1925–1970*
(New York: Grove Press, 1974).

Search the earth.
Some of us never stretch the circumference
Neruda flew around the world
like light, and still had time
to dance with lions,
speak wisdom to the sun,
admire the legs of women,
leap fences with children and antelope,
plant songs in the trenches of Santiago,

His words

> like the stride of strong thighs
> the nostrils of horses mating
> the blood of women bearing
> the shoulders of soldiers embattled
> the hands of a fiddler, singing

Don't ask
where is the love poem

> Look . . . he is in the streets
> "ready to sing or to die."

WE, THE DANGEROUS

I swore
it would not devour me
I swore
it would not humble me
I swore
it would not break me.

    And they commanded we dwell in the desert
    Our children be spawn of barbed wire and barracks

We, closer to the earth,
squat, short thighed,
knowing the dust better.

    And they would have us make the garden
    Rake the grass to soothe their feet

We, akin to the jungle,
plotting with the snake,
tails shedding in civilized America.

    And they would have us skin their fish
    deft hands like blades/sliding back flesh/bloodless

We, who awake in the river
Ocean's child
Whale eater.

    And they would have us strange scented women,
    Round shouldered/strong and yellow/like the moon
    to pull the thread to the cloth
    to loosen their backs massaged in myth

We, who fill the secret bed,
the sweat shops
the launderies.

And they would dress us in napalm,
Skin shred to clothe the earth,
Bodies filling pock marked fields.
Dead fish bloating our harbors.

We, the dangerous,
Dwelling in the ocean.
Akin to the jungle.
Close to the earth.

Hiroshima
Vietnam
Tule Lake

And yet we were not devoured.
And yet we were not humbled
And yet we are not broken.

SPOILS OF WAR

(excerpt)

She could barely breathe, the desire was so heavy, like the weight of a wave, wafting her around in a vast sea. He was very blond, very blue and very sure of himself. Their lovemaking was wet, heaving. His weight on her pressed her deep into a place she thought she had dreamed about a long time ago.

The grasses grew high during the early spring. Lupines, deep purple, swung by the wind like a wave of dancers. The smell was so sweet, she thought she could pluck and eat. The color deep like pools in sleeves of stored kimonos. She wove the full stems into a wreath. "Don't wear live flowers, or there will be death in the family," her mother warned.

She would slip them into the throat of her grandmother's lap, as she rocked in her silent timelessness. Grandma, always rocking, as if to nurse memories of another place. The family all vied and competed for her—she was magic, glowing from her quiet secret of peace. When grandma died, she felt a deep guilt.

The men were a silent, commanding presence . . . wordless except for spurts of hostility and occasional glowing threats of violence. Perhaps because of the inflexible will of these men, bound tightly within, giving nothing of their deep selves for the women to nurture, that the women had little to reflect themselves. The cycle perpetuated was isolation/surface blank mirrors/unspoken seethings.

What she knew best was the steady, controlled progression to survive, like the turning of a slow wheel.

She longed for the intensity of verbal presence . . . but he tried to maneuver her into the bed. His impatient need, the words to get more, get more.

The distance he created after it was over drove her to perform strange soundings: turmoil, dependency, exotic addition. She didn't even know how she did it, turning on her side, weeping. Telling him of the deep hurt he would inflict. And he would appease, weakly.

What he represented . . . a power only they possessed . . . that they could turn minds into libraries, laboratories, brick buildings, bombs.

Somewhere in the back of her being she was awed. They could demolish an entire people and no one questioned their supreme authority to do so. The people, whom she knew in her mind, and had been able to feel the edges of their reality through grandparents, were somehow mystically related to sea creatures. She saw how when they became dangerous, they were destroyed. But still, Japan was just a name. Like "parent." Like "camps." Like "Issei, Nisei, Sansei, Yonsei."

Birth by Fire.

"Burn it." Yuki said, eyes flowing like spigots. Hard wet eyes, determined to see the red silk wrapping the emblem, the dense character filled, folded scrolls for the last time. Destroy by fire. "So they don't find any trace of home here. Burn it." The fire leapt and swallowed paper, silk, even porcelain. Flames yellowed as the last strand melted. That day, only the sounds of fire's final licking, the dying, sucked the densely quiet room. Yuki's womb still draining hot afterbirth.

Bundles, knotted tightly, quickly, some left behind, heavy like the bodies lifting them to the truck taking them to the depot. Signs, posted on the door, flapped like an obscene wing, waving farewell:

"instructions to all persons of Japanese ancestry persuant to the provisions of Civilian Exclusion Order No. 33, dated April 22, 1942, all persons of Japanese ancestry both alien and non alien will be evacuated . . ."

Yuki, her bundles, boarded the train, infant in arms. Sachiko, her eight year old niece, trailed behind her, pulling her coat, a tag like those used to mark luggage, tied around her neck. Eyes cold. No longer flowing, lips pressed as the infant writhed in hunger, tightly screaming, Yuki sat. "Burn it," she whispered as the train steamed to start. Bodies, familiar . . . Sachiko, Okasan, Otosan, limply rocked like the bundles in the motion of the train. Silent weeping whispered to the rhythm of its wheels. Sachiko was gagging.

She flopped properly when Gerald fucked her, pressing her deep within herself, until she was transformed into that which his weight would define. She didn't think she cared about climax, only that he thought she had it. She was caught somewhere between the spoken complaint and the need to be opaque. Others had told her and Gerald repeated: you are not inadequate because of anything the others say, but because you are. You make it so, inherently.

Yuki watched out the window. Another time, though time blurred like the trees, hills, specks of animals the train left behind. Chicago to California. California to Tule Lake.

Her child, now five, crumpled next to her, bag over her mouth, gagging steadily from motion sickness all the way from Illinois to Utah. Her new husband slept across from her, mouth open in his snoring. He was no comfort. Already in their short time of marriage he began to change, now openly cruel to the child. She was dazed at his apparent hatred toward it. Because it was ugly—"Look, those eyes, puffed up folds. Teeth rolling out."

She felt the desert in her bones. And it frightened her so she clung to him to hide the dread, the darkening yawn of emptiness. She thought it would be better if they moved to California. It would be alright now since the war was over for a few years. They wouldn't be so cruel to them, as memory and hatred grew dimmer. He would be able to feel freer, perhaps his pride less hurt on the farm, relatively independent. It's better to owe her parents than be owned by a company, they rationalized.

How long ago, this same feeling. The train, and this desolation. This child, an infant in my arms. Sachiko next to me, gagging. Swallow the vomit. There are so many people. Shame on shame. Sickness, the smell, the red swollen faces from so much crying. Rigid resignation. Trees fading, wind and sand blowing. Sage scattered like skeletons. Clouds like ghosts mocking in the dry, dry, heat.

She didn't have the strength to be sympathetic anymore. The child would mercifully sleep for several hours, wake up gagging over her mother's skirt. How much more can she get up? No food for days. She was getting so weak, flopping like a cloth over her mother's lap. They both hung in the motion of the train, speeding through the endless flats of salt.

How familiar, my skin feeling the airless wind. The smell of vomit all around me. Then the barracks spiking the ground. Wondering what the crime. My infant, wet, weak from the journey. Rash breaking from her face. A rush to the crudely constructed toilets. Guards looking through us. And the stall-less places. Strangers looking on my crouching nakedness. Red humiliation cloaking me. The smell of naked piss.

Don't you think it wrong to be so pompous? Cold? Critical? Keeping me isolated? Weakened by guilt. Her feeble attempts to define herself were unheard, perhaps because they were mouthed with little resolve.

The weakness was reinforced somehow by the ever opening of her thighs, the hungry tight closing around him as he pressed her deeply into the bed.

As long as she could remember, she did not exist. There was physical body, thin legs and arms, small torso, flat hips, and a face that changed as often as the reactions to it. There was a thing they did praise . . . the length and shape of her thighs. Otherwise, she was flat, faceless.

She remembered the childhood make believe names she and her friend, Junko, adopted when their families lived in adjoining apartments in the tenement on lower south side Chicago. She hated her own name. And they would dream together of escape from endless clotheslines, the taunting boys whose haircuts were shaped like bowls. Her mother, the fair skinned, untouchable, "beautiful one" was a shadow to her, who cried in anger when she'd tantrum for attention. Yuki floated in and out of her daughter's life with many suitors. The handsome Haru brought flowers until they got married. He would even woo the daughter.

She could understand why any man would court her mother. Yuki seemed created to have a man take care of the delicate, snow like beauty. After their marriage, Haru brought them west to the farm, where her mother worked like a man.

She imagined Yuki was only happy when she was in bed with Haru. She complained a lot otherwise. In the early evening, sometimes she'd see a happy glaze over her mother's eyes. Those times, late at night, she'd be awakened by the suppressed moan, the whispers of Haru: "Yuki, kimochi eh." The tender calm of those moments, hearing the closeness of bodies, she would feel the strange stir in herself, where the thighs met, and she'd be ashamed of the wet and toss herself to sleep.

Yuki would catch Haru staring at the young girl's developing body, fuller busted, elongated, articulate.

When the daughter first bled, frightened, ashamed, Yuki told her it was because she was thinking too much about forbidden things, and she must not let any man kiss her or she would become pregnant. Her schoolmates laughed at her for weeks when she repeated that horror to them.

The perimeters of her being were defined by the growing shape of her flesh. Use it well, she was told and she would know happiness.

When Gerald fondled her, his hands were oppressive, too present, but his eyes were someplace else. Not seeing, but watching as she groaned in the right tone, closed her eyes in feigned ecstasy. He kneaded her breasts as if they could rise, as she heaved herself up. He would bring himself to release and leave her to shower.

She would try to talk to him of Spinoza, Augustine and British law, but it bored her, and he could conduct monologues for hours. "Politics is simply a transient reflection of society's mood . . . frivolous, predictable, shallow. Without immutable law, humans would be reduced to irrational barbarians. War, for example, is a logical manifestation of the irrational nature of man. And for man, all is fair in war." She wished he would hold her again.

The train became a part of her. It breathed for her. Whatever it felt, Yuki felt. The belly of her child, heaving. The belly of the train rancid. California was a dream. A place/blurred with the smell of vomit, as she had boarded the other train to another desert place.

Sachiko gagging. Sachiko of the ready smile, quick to comfort, sensitive to the others' hurt, making infants laugh with her laughter, lifting even Ojichan from his gloom, with antics commanding joy.

Guardtowers held young men, barely men. Rifled. Helmets hiding their eyes. They were there a long time.

One day, Ojichan went to the barbed fence, looking for pieces of wood to carve, forgetting the forbidden closeness to the gate. When he stooped to grasp the wood, the boy in the tower abruptly drew his rifle. Yuki gasped. Sachiko suddenly slid to him, laughter loud. Pulled him from the fence, "you will make me a fine Daruma from that." Ojichan, smiling, not noticing the soldier's frightened aim, led back to life by Sachiko. Yuki wanted to cry like an infant, her own in her arms, squirming for her breastmilk.

Immutable law . . . "the consequences of law are unquestionable. Debatable, but unquestionable," Gerald droned, "one can question the morality of warfare, especially nuclear, but one cannot deny that the dropping of the A-bomb in Japan ended the war unconditionally . . . they surrendered. And isn't that the bottom line? to win, regardless."

"They had made peace overtures before the bomb was dropped, I read . . ." she interjected. "But war doesn't justify any country being used as America's laboratory . . ."

"Atrocity is inconsequential. People forget," he huffed. "My Lai is also called an atrocity, but in the context of the situation, is a means to an end. Besides, in World War II, we would have had to share the spoils of war with Russia if we didn't drop . . ." His face swelled with a smile.

"The spoils of war . . ." she began to weep.

"You're too emotional. Each event has a matching mark in history . . . there is nothing new under the sun . . ."

Then there is no hope for me, she thought.

Words like a wall, keeping her out, locking her in. Words choking her in the face of something so wrong. Empty space between the space of letters in her head. Win. Profit. Human life inconsequential. They would not surrender. All is fair in war . . . Do the people know what the generals weave?

Gerald ceased fire for the night. Lifting her to the demilitarized zone. Pulled the bedcover. She, drowning in a wave of sheets, surrendering to dark sleep:

> The road shimmered across farmlands in the heat.
>
> Three families managed the farms, and expanded little by little, though they were poor and had to start over on their land after the war.
>
> Everyone was irritable today because of the heat wave, unrelenting, windless.
>
> All the children wanted to play across the road where the creek ran, the cool relief of that shaded place, willows hanging like they'd been there forever. Even they drooped more.
>
> The children loved to catch tadpoles in the spring, and in the heavy summer months, when the frogs were everywhere, they caught them in jars, fed them dragonflies.
>
> The water was a magic place where fantasies became real. The stream carrying her to the sea, where she played like a mermaid, singing in the sun, traveling continents, speaking strange tongues, scaling new mountains, plunging new depths, dancing in the holiness of music.
>
> Today, with the heat stabbing their skin, the children begged to go to their creek. Her cousin, dark eyed, blossom lipped Sachiko, thin, quick, short straight bangs whipping as she ran, was scolded for her impatience. She was older, about 14, and always leading the others, laughing as she danced with the pebbles on the path to the creek.
>
> The road was a freeway to another large town, and traffic was always too fast. They were cautioned frequently.
>
> Sachiko broke from the younger cousins, eager to get to the cool shade. The screaming of brakes pierced the dense heat. Everyone ran, suddenly chilled, hoping it was a chicken, a dog or another small animal they often saw split by the tires of speeding cars. The children

were stopped near the open gate to the road. All the adults ran down the road quite a ways where the car had veered crazily and stopped.

Afterward, Yuki, tears choking, told them Sachiko had been thrown so far it took them a few minutes to find her. Her thin legs, like the stalks of grass jutting from the ground on the side of the road.

"We should have taken it." Haru almost shouted.

Startled, Yuki looked up slowly, her red eyes burning with more than grief. "$200.00?" she almost hissed. "We'll see," Haru said. "We'll see what the courts do for a hakujin and what they do for us." His jaw was working tightly, as he jarred out of the room.

She thought she would suffocate in the room full with the women's sobs, their grief shrouding the walls. Death was a stranger to her then.

She sat up in the darkness. Gerald grunted softly and stirred, turned on his side. Her skin prickled as she felt the terrible emptiness of air on her arms. "Without the law, humans would be reduced . . ."

Attorney Magnusen said they should not sue. Costly, lengthy for an accident. Settle out of court.

Incense circling over Sachiko's coffin. Silent lines of mourners. Chants and white paper over flowers. She was held as they viewed the body. Sachiko looked older lying there. She reached out a hand to stroke the pale cheek. Suddenly she was very afraid.

The family got nothing from the man who said he was not drunk when his car hit the kid. She came from nowhere he had said, like a chicken flying across the road.

Law, mutable by the makers.

The days of her life flew on. She was panicking because she would soon finish her degree. Somehow she couldn't face the end of this phase of her life. The institution kept her snug in its rigidity, its walls promising to keep everything the same until she could find the strength to move on, tomorrow. There were practical problems like money. And she was bored with the menial jobs. Maybe she could use the sociology. Gerald encouraged her to get a Ph.D. The relationship certainly had no feeling of progression, but it was one she would rather kill than break or change.

The world he wanted to keep her in was sufficiently isolated and protective of his values that she would continue to receive the same realities . . . brick on brick, the tomb was still attractive.

She went for an interview for a part-time summer position at the Community Counseling Service. The black man who sat behind his disarrayed desk was muscular, animated, his flesh shining as he talked and smiled. She was aware of the look he gave her as their conversation coursed through many subjects, and she wanted to draw closer. When he asked her to dinner, she lowered her eyes, a technique she had learned. Busy tonight or anytime? Wanting to keep him near, but not too near, she looked at her hands.

His eyes flashed, and her blood sang with fear, excitement, dread. It depends . . . she started.

"On whether you get this job or not?" he interrupted. Her mouth was open, caught. "You intellectual broads are all the same. Same game, same line, same pose."

The sinking feeling of losing herself again . . . it had something to do with guilt.

Her uncle offered her a walk through the field. It was dark. She had stayed at her grandmother's too long. She welcomed the offer. In the hot night, toads were thick on the dust dry stretch where the corn had been cut. She dreaded stepping on them. Obscene croaks. He held the flashlight so she could see the toads parting the path, his free arm on her shoulders. Flashlight clicked off. The ground silently leaping around her. Thoughts of escape. No courage to step through the toads. Nervous laugh. Feeble shove. Darkness like toads, swallows wandering insects.

After bathing, she approached Yuki, still shaken and asked why her uncle would want to touch her in that way. Her mother rose up with a surprising rage . . . "What did you do . . ." "he wouldn't do that unless . . ." Her young body quivered in a strange abstract guilt, not understanding but certain her mother spoke with a knowledge that came from some experience of her own. Blushing, she tried to protest, but her mother was lost to her. Her rage turned cold, as the child shivered in the wake of accusations.

Woman. victim? violator? perpetrator? The conspiracy.

"Don't you have it turned around," she began to protest.

His face grew darker: "you use your body like your mind. A lot of pages of books that you can quote, memorized. You can't even field a hit. You probably have some steps you've memorized for a *meaningful relationship*, so you don't have to fuck. really fuck. You have *intercourse*. All up there. You won't cop to your responsibility . . ."

"Who do you think . . ."

"You come in here for a job, lead the game, spout sociological garbage and pretend it ain't happening." His eyes burned with an anger she knew nothing about. It frightened her. But she couldn't leave. Something made her stay, and they talked. They talked.

He stood up, over her, pulled her up from her chair, gently, and held her for some moments.

Fingers burning. Flesh searing. His warmth reaching. He was honest and it touched a deep need she did not know she had. Her life built on mistrust and fear. His directness attracting/repelling her. She felt herself fade again, not able to keep her presence in his embrace. The flame he built in her she washed with denial. When he pulled her face to his, she turned away, the old vacuum creeping into her belly.

Suddenly, he pulled her hair back. Whispered protests. Small fists whipping, pushing. He humped over her, containing movement. His mouth opened. Loud laugh. He fully clothed. Laughing as he released her, she struggled with the clothing, choking crimson, weak with humiliation. He was still laughing . . . "Better go Home . . ." as she vanished.

Yuki, Haru stood like flames before the yawning black square of Sachiko's grave. They flickered in the sunset, shoulders firm as if to hold back final statements. She stood between them, feeling their pillar strength. She quieted at Haru's iron set face.

Going home from the cemetery, Haru spoke gently to Yuki, "Sorry I asked you to take the money." That was one of the few times she ever heard "sorry" from him.

"We'll fight, Yuki. Magnusen isn't the only attorney around. Too bad Yas isn't in California. He'd show that judge something." Uncle Yas, Haru's brother who finished first in law school and practicing in Chicago.

His voice rose in controlled fury, addressing something beyond Yuki. "We can't give up. Too much too long."

Yuki was sobbing, wet words streaming . . . "How much suffering."

"What good does that do? Suffering forever. What matters is how you bear it when it happens. We won't be broken. Besides. It never stopped when we were quiet."

She had not heard such a clear, focused fire. The car seared the road, spinning through Haru's hurt, crushing the brush that blew across his path. She knew she mustn't speak. It is that pride when violated that flares and threatens everything around it. And she thrilled in the beauty of its strength.

They fought. The new lawyer was indifferent, they said, and he didn't push for anything. But they fought. Each day, Haru would wear a tie he hated, and his best jacket; Yuki would put on her suit, and they'd go with Sachiko's parents to the court. Each day, they returned. Drained, firm lipped. Haru holding all of them tightly in his determination.

She would catch Yuki looking at him, her face open, admiring. Yuki knew he was set to get what he wanted. Even though their weariness told them the case was lost, she felt Haru steadily fight even those who had given up, to win the suit against the man he called murderer.

Case dismissed.

Haru spoke no more of it. But hurt glistened from him like a tree wearing rain.

Don't forget from where you have come. Don't desert dignity to endure. Don't abandon the struggle to shape your own soul.

The sound of his laugh burning in her being. Something she knew she did. The collusion with the game. And she was left faceless. He had stripped her of even her body... the only means of her definition. He exposed, lay bare, revealed fully, and finally rejected the empty shell. The deceptions upon which she had built her life.

Refusal to take responsibility. Making herself victim was the punishment. Self fulfilling destruction. She walked for a long time into the evening not knowing the direction.

> *Visions of famine*
> *like trees*
> *burned from a fist of flame*
> *I wander from village*
> *to village*
> *asking stalks of people*
> *who stare with eyes*
> *hollow from too much light.*
> *Where is home?*
> *Silence follows me*
> *like the clouds.*
> *Answer please.*

The ground rises
with a terrible swell
of smells from bodies
buried in her.

She found herself by the beach. The water thundering in her. The rage of foam spat on her face as she thought again, again, of the man today, the erection on her chest as she lay on the floor, pinned like an insect who had come too close to the flame.

Arashi	*Storm wind*
fuku	*blows*
	ocean waves outstretched
	clutching for the moon.

Her mind tossed, something in her ribs searing. Foam like fingers reaching for her thighs. Seaweed spread like strands of a dying woman. Flame growing. She had not cried like this before. Water streaming from her shoulders.

Ame	*Rain Rain*
Ame furu	*dressing the flame*
	in strands of
	silver

She shivered and ran to the rain cleaned streetlights. She wanted to curl up in the safe, predictable place of Gerald's weight. At least it was something she could touch . . . turmoil follows, everywhere.

That night, as he held her in the foam of sheets, t.v. blasting, she looked into the mouth of night and saw the electronic vision clearly before her. Between gasps of the fucking. T.V. droning

Nixon, nose skiing to the corners of his jaws, fingering long stems of microphones, pumping with fists for emphasis . . . "it is necessary to escalate penetration into enemy harbors. These communists stop at nothing . . . spread like maggots in a democracy clean world . . ."

She longed to draw him closer, closer . . . as if driven to experience the depths of torture. She cast away her own body, plummeting the emptiness, scaling the strange new pain.

"of course Lt. Calley was acting in the line of duty.
. . . necessary to show we mean business."

Gerald stroking her flesh.

"napalm is a success . . . their surrender imminent . . ."

mounting her again, pressing breath from her.

"my fellow americans . . . the spoils of war . . ."

as he entered/grinding deep within her

"we'll bomb them to the peace table . . ."

releasing without thought to her reaching

electronic eyes following the pumping bodies, sweat popping,
"victory at all cost . . ."

The sick feeling spread to her arms, as she clawed his shoulder to
dismount. This was not desire. Her shape changed/defined by the slit
she needed filled. filled.

> Umi   Ocean
> Kagami   mirror of the night
>   show me nothing.
>   Everything.

Gerald took her to a dinner party given by friends, "very influential
with the bar association." chic, glib, society's elite. Stiff discomfort for
her. Gerald smiling a lot. Indifferent conversations on war, politicians,
My lai, cuisine. Voices raised in consternation, intense, angry voices on
the injustice toward ducks . . . victims of oil. Angry indignation about
whales and jap whalers.

> Kujira   whales sounding
> ochite   where did the fish hide
>   when the water
>   filled with death's light

They say the worst way to go is by drowning. Slow. Except for unforeseen attacks, where weeks, years after the mushroom cloud people vomited up their life.

She remembered the helpless flock of chickens, scattered by the slightest sound. Her heart felt like that, flying across the road in the path of crushing tires. Not able to take flight, splattered on dead asphalt.

The scavengers feasted.

1941 newsflashes. Boycott Japan. "The question was how we should maneuver Japan into firing the first shot without allowing too much danger to ourselves . . . we have provoked war . . ." stated the secretary of war.

Flame in her fueling. All is fair in war. flame rising, bone burning. Mushroom clouds flashing.

"We do live from the ocean," laughed Mr. Hashimoto. His gentle laugh warming his customers when he came with his truck. All the Japanese American farmers called it the "ark" because it connected them to each other. He delivered foodstuffs from Japan they couldn't buy anywhere in the predominantly white nearby towns.

Octopus, dried shrimp, kamabuko, unagi, real rice, fresh tofu— everything they craved for their diets. The women, all the children, even sometimes Haru, would run out to greet Hashimoto-san, rejoicing in his Wednesday visits.

They would not only get their essential food supplies, but the latest news about the Yamaguchi's new baby, the crop failure of the Shimizus, the illness of Mrs. Arai, the big catch of trout by Mr. Asaki. Mr. Hashimoto would be an hour or so late sometimes because he would be so busy conveying good wishes, get wells, and good lucks exchanged between the farmer families in the vast area he covered with his truck.

Yuki said, "He's such a good man," when they couldn't pay up their bills some weeks, and he would cheerfully whisper, "next time."

When Hashimoto-san became ill, his color paled, his smile dimmed. They would give him gifts, home remedies, tell him to slow down. Still he came every week, knowing they could not get their food from home . . .

She thought she would never forget Mr. Hashimoto's smile, and the fish smells from his wonderful ark.

Provoke war, tramping to the rhythm of her footsteps. The scattered plates of food thrown at the shocked dinner party still sticking on her shoes. She couldn't remember the words spuming from her at the doughfaced gathering, but she knew she wouldn't be seeing him/them again.

> Action is the name
> for hope.

She had walked very far. The streetlights in the fog were an eerie runway. dangerous for flight. ready for flight. Her face burned into shape. Her nameless face tingling in the fog, mixed with salt.

> Gold flesh shouts
> remember me.
> Colors were so vivid
> in her other eye.
> Crimson walls and live
> flowers jumping from
> her mother's throat
> barbed wire crowning her hair.
> Little by little
> she remembers the shadow
> of herself
> dancing in the presence
> of flowers,
> grandmother,
> and the language of the sea.
> Yuki, nodding,
> as blood
> flows from her forehead
> waving goodbye,
> my nameless child.
> Wear live flowers
> in your hair—you will die.
> Live again
> in a new time
> and send me
> back yourself.

The cold, like the hate she felt for herself, retreated from her blood. Pumping another song. She wished she could talk to Haru, just once, and let him know what she let herself remember.

She called Haru, "Papa." Always came in after dark from the work . . . his weariness like a coat he slowly shed as Yuki brought him hot tea. He had beautiful arms, lean, taut. Long arms that lifted heavy sacks of grain. She thought he must be very strong, because he carried them without straining, carefully, like a body.

Those sacks of grain. Like gold. No. food for life. She would have to go to the stockroom, and sweep up any that had spilled, carefully like coins. No. food for life.

The man with the red, beefy face, with the stomach shaped like a pear, would come every week to collect the bill for the grain. He'd stand around, eyes shifting at Yuki's behind, until Papa came out; then he'd laugh, holding out his hand.

Papa never shook his hand. She never told him how proud that made her.

She had heard that when a child is about to be born, the family hangs blue fish to insure the birth of sons. She wondered how blue the fish before her birth.

> *Water reaching*
> *foam spraying*
> *the shape of man*
> *of our race/emerging*
> *without fins.*
> *Where have you been?*
> *Looking to a faceless mirror*
> *I have hated you*
> *father, turning away from me.*
> *My need for your love*
> *so deep*
> *you, out of reach*
> *like this sea*
> *that circles the world*
> *to the place that is home.*
> *Gold skinned men*
> *firm lipped men*

black eyed, silent
men—touch me.
Turning, turning
from myself
i could not see you—
dust covered hands
pain wracked pride
sweat tracked backs
muscles popping from the weight.
Dignity is to be unbroken
i did not hear your strength unspoken.
Love deep/hurt deeper,
we destroy
before we change.
Love spreads like the shoreline
crumbles everything
even the great rocks
of hate we sculpt.

Wave on wave, the ocean stretched for her, linking her to a place she would slowly remember . . . "better go home . . ."

Home was changed, new. Yuki, Haru standing like strong trees in a yellow sunrise.

She, no longer faceless. Barefaced. The ocean raged, but she was not the helpless vessel tossed. She was the foam

the ocean's hew
dancing in the sanctity
of its sound,
circling full
around.

In the deep cave of night she called, contrapuntal to the water's cry, My Name is Hatsuko.

Never be faceless
and silent
when you are near
the shore that
is your own strange song.

A SONG FOR YOU

for Cecil

You laugh
your big laugh
your hands
      like wings
      or a dancer's wish
enclosures for the last/first sleep

I want to
hold
suck
taste your skin
breathing in
that dark, deep

I want to
bathe your limbs
like trees
your roots
entangled hard in mine

and walk your back
from Tokyo
to Dar Es Salaam
lulling you with genmai tea

touch me
sing me
make me born
together we will
sound lost bones
and color their flesh

yes,
we will hold
the sea
you and i
and bring
the deep/moist/soft
mouth
to the shores
of all
our continents.

LULLABYE

My mother merely shakes
her head
when we talk about the war,
the camps,
the bombs.

She won't discuss
the dying/her own
as she left her self
with the stored belongings.

She wrapped her shell
in kimono sleeves
and stamped it third class
delivery to Tule Lake

> *futokoro no ko*
> > *child at my breast*
> *oya no nai*
> > *parentless*

What does it mean to be citizen?

> *It is privilege*
> *to pack only what you can carry*

> *It is dignity*
> *to be interned for your own good*

> *It is peace of mind*
> *constituted by inalienable right*

She x'd the box mark "other"

pledging allegiance
to those who would have turned
on the gas mercifully

Her song:
shikata ga nai
    it can't be helped

She rode on the train
destined for omission
with an older cousin

who died next to her
gagging when her stomach burned out.

Who says you only die once?

My song:

Watashi ga kadomo wa matte eru
I am a child waiting
        waiting
Watashi no hahaga umareta
    for the birth of my mother.

THE FISHERMAN

Ojichan was a fisherman/farmer
more a fisherman,
cleaning his bait
winding his line,
the smell of sardines
seeping from his sea-cracked hands.
The muscles of his face spoke
but his tongue silent
except for syllables
of survival
         sake
         oi ocha
         kata o momu
and obachan would
knead the strong knots
on his shoulders.
Only when he put on his boots
and left the house for China Lake
pipe cocked in his mouth
a certain way,
there seemed a light
from his straightened frame
eyes noisy,
muscles in a little dance.
And when he came home,
laughing as he fished his catch
from the depths of his box,
gloated that his old friend
Kinjo caught only one,
and set the stiff rainbow
pearled fish
out for the women to scale,
wide mouths gaping
surprised eyes encorpsing
the room.

Many nights
over sake
making guttural sounds
with Kinjo,
the light from him was brighter.
           That winter
China Lake was
cold, winds shaped water
into hands, fingers
clawed the shore
No one else would go
but Kinjo
rocking years and pride
rowed out with his son.
The boat turned
like a small fish
The old man
went down
water freezing in his bones.
His son reached for him,
dived two times
did not come up again.
The people
stood on the dock
and looked.
           I think it hurt Ojichan
deeply
Kinjo fished from China Lake.
           After,
he would sit
looking into the sun,
body dimmed
muscles knotted
eyes silent.
He wore his loss like his heavy boots,
legs moving
in slow underwater motion
when he learned how they
stood and looked
and did nothing.

ATTACK THE WATER

Juxtaposition of war photos
and news flashes, 1942/1972

My first flash
on the newsprint/face
she could have been
Obachan
back then/just after
the camps
when the land/dried/up

no water for months.

In town,
they would not sell
to japs.

We had to eat what
we could grow
that's only natural.

We ate rice with roots.

                                    Vietnamese woman
her face etched old
by newsprint/war
mother/grandmother
she has beared them all

(have they all died?)

            Flash!!
"they are bombing the waterways . . .

"this new offensive
which has previously/been/ avoided/
for//humanitarian//reasons/
will/seriously/jeopardize
their//food//situation!!"

Obachan
sitting
breathing heavily
in the sun
watching her pet rabbits
(she loved them like children)

which one

tonight?

I still remember her eyes
drawing the blood
like water.

And the rice—
there were maggots
in the rice.

no water
to flush/them/out.

Up river
bodies floated in My Chanh
eyes eaten by crabs
flushed onto the land—

fly food.

*"They/are/attacking the water/
when all else fails
Attack the Water."*

Obachan
would chew
the food first/spit
out maggots.

Grandchildren
ate
the spit-flushed rice.

      When all else fails
      attack the water.

WHEN SHE ENTERS

for D . . .

When she sings
with her eyes, the room
dances and her earrings loop
trances around the moon of her face.
Brown skinned/jade fingers
cymbals on her tongue.
And all the brothers
are captured
in the fine flare of her nostrils.
She sways,
whispers
i love you
to each in the silent
breathing of her hems.
And everyone
wants
to make her their own
even just for the night.
It is like
holding your own cheetah
gazelle with a lion's soul
pacing that sensual pace
when encaged.
Feel the secret power
to contain
the wild pacing/you
can't tame.
She will kill you
if she can
any second now
escape/maul/enflame
but you love the
pain
even more
knowing you can't keep her.

DROWNING IN THE YELLOW RIVER

Necking in back seats

of convertibles with white boys
while elvis
creams out your pain

               screams out your song
               "you ain't nothin' but a . . ."

who else am i?

The silk scarf obachan
gave you
you wear like ann margaret
in convertible winds

               flapping to
               "don't step on my . . ."

who else am i?

look at me—
buddaheads
chinamen who stand
on one side of the room
and don't mess with girls

who else am i?

necking is so hard
in the back seat
with white boys
had to pee so bad
crossing your legs

               elvis panting
               "don't be cruel"

she couldn't say
stop suckin' on my neck daddy-o
gotta go
to the obenjo

                              one once asked if jap toilets
                              had horizontal plumbing

who else am i?

crossing your legs
slid the silk scarf
into your crotch

                              elvis stops for a commercial
                              "wonder where the yellow went . . ."

obachan's silk scarf
sucked the yellow river
you came home
rumpled
hickied

(he'll call you again sometime)

you hung
your yellowed
pee-drowned scarf to dry

who else am i?

BREATHE BETWEEN THE RAIN

For Bayani & Serafin, poets
who live among us still.

We, gathered in this place
stars like eyes
watching our words
How many in our numbers?

> We lost Bayani
> that day
> his soul flying
> before him
> eager to fathom the light
> flesh twitching
> from a spirit's kiss
> He saw too deep
> to stay among us.

And

> Serafin
> pain bundled
> between his eyes
> bursting through his veins
> like his love
> he left us
> with an ache
> that would last forever
> and visions of manongs
> as beautiful as carabao
> lifting their necks
> to the wind.

Count our numbers.
Don't mourn losses too long
or it will render us useless
like vessels emptied.

Listen instead to the song
their legacy of strength.
We can circle our own
ritual,
make language,
new words, rooted in our bones.

A dance
to bear us to safety
muscling strong.
Listen to their song
rhyming with survival
teach our children
that nothing is more precious
than human life.
Count our numbers.

> We lost Minoru
> when they came to take us
> died of shame
> in Topaz
> died of shame

know our true enemy.

> We lost Shigemi
> hiding in the tall stems
> of yellow flowers
> they even shot
> off the heads of chrysanthemums

Count our numbers.
harvest our strength.
breathe between the rain.
We shall not go into their camps again.

The dirt beneath the graves will speak
From between our thighs will come new tribes.

SEPTEMBER SECOND

On the Victory of the People of
Vietnam. To Mrs. Huong

It is the second of September
the leaves are turning
red tinges the edges
like fingers dripping.
There has been much blood
sucked by our mother
the earth
she has received your children.
I will not forget your face
as you spoke of them
interning them in our minds
describing their lovely eyes
as the cages bled their life.
Each day/as the sun mourned,
the crazy fire
dropped by the enemy
branded their infamy.
It is the second of September
I hope you are well
the sun warming your face
as you visit your children's graves
your hands rebuilding the earth
the sun will repair
one day.

    You, i remember
as you have been burned in my listening body
I long to hear you
speak of this day
the earth rejoicing
with the sound of your songs

It is the second of September
and the wind
touching the arms
of trees
leaves/bleeding
we will not forget
your many children/Vietnam.

It is the second of September
and the wind is marching
blowing the leaves like banners
singing through our bodies
clothing the earth like a spirit
marching
victorious
I am with you
my sister
and my tears
wash gladly
as I see you/glimmering
alive/free.

A LECHEROUS POEM TO TOSHIRO MIFUNE

The sound of
shakuhachi
is oozing around my mind.
Beautiful
samurai/rebel
squared in the snow
with eye-blinking speed
sliced the wind
and opponent,
blood bursting the cold air.
His woman is looking on
in the high field
breasts heaving
obi flying
He squares his back
arms hidden
shoulders keeping time
to his leaving
her behind.
Toshiro, you don't ever get down
with your women
why don't you?
I can really get into you
sitting in that room alone,
sifting the thoughts of your
ancients,
mind and body
one with your sword
but
must you scorn her
all the time?
Don't misunderstand—
I really dig
that ritual—
that clear, clean
blade of discipline,

that taut wire
connected with my ancestors,
that gathering of all time
into moment beyond all time
that put/feeling/aside
one/ness/with/nature/self

perfectly in tune
         like the

              "bell ringing in an empty sky"

         like the

              flute crying alone

         like the

              sound of sun on stone.

And oh, Mifune,
you are so fine
I can sit with you for hours
and wait
and wait
for that climax
for that instant whipping of your blade

ckhhhhhhhaaaap!

but as you walk off
in the wind blown lonely
twilight,
without even looking back
your high
wide
stepping in time
to japanese/cowboy music,

i am
that woman
kimono clad
silent and motionless
(except for heaving breast)
suppressing all the frustation/emptiness
not wanting that loneliness

i am
that hair tearing
hara-kiri prone/
longing/licking
body-burning-for-you
woman of the dunes.

Turn around Mifune!!

stop cleaning your blade.

we can make

an eternity

together.

THE QUESTION IS

Yellow is
the color of lemons,
sun,
early morning on water.

I, with other thoughts,
encounter you—
your blue eyes
dissolving with doubtful words of love,
whispering to me:

> You are so
> exotic
> so curiously pale

> Your Kind
> has always attracted me

> Your slanted eyes
> hold mysteries of the orient

> Give me
> your novelty body.

> But before you do
> the Question
> Is
> it true
> your cunt is slanted too?

CRAZY ALICE

Aunt Alice, who has touched the sun . . .
victim of American Concentration Camps

She came to the
wedding
in a tattered coat
called us all by
the wrong names

Yukio/Mizume/Kyoko

No, crazy Alice
We died in the camps

                    remembering/remembering
                    Alice/back then

and the relatives
laughed behind
her back/crazy Alice

                    the bride is beautiful
                    who is she?

crazy Alice
it is your daughter

                    okashi ne
                    jinsei wa okashi

                    life's so strange
                    before the war
                    i had a name

twenty years ago
she would come to us
face blue
eyes like black walnuts
and down her nose
blood flowed like tears

battered by husbands
and lovers
for hoarding food
and love

where has love gone?

        the children
        will starve
        remember the war
        eating potato roots

and thinking of
invasions
and prison camps
she opened her legs
to the white boss man

        okashi ne
        jinsei wa okashi

        life's so strange
        before the war
        i had a name

crazy Alice
where do you wander?
you walk on the sun
your eyes
keep the years
motionless
and your tears like rain
on a sleeping sea

        my child is hungry
        what will i do

crazy Alice
    crazy Alice

she is the bride
standing before you

my child is dead
my breasts dried
during the war
and she died
from hunger

rejoice
Crazy Alice/your child
has a new name

okashi ne, okashi
Jinsei wa okash:

life's so strange
before the war
i was my child
i had a name.

CANTO A NERUDA

I among men bear the same wounded hand
suffer the same reddened cup
and live an identical rage.

Pablo Neruda

Mountains are
crying
in shame

Rivers are outraged

Cities crumble
from the people's
pain

> This was Vietnam
> Chile's anguish
> Mindanao

> Blood crosses oceans
> floods the streets.

Flesh tightened on bones
Flesh washed by blood
Flesh gutted by flies.

With so many friends already
dead
and others who will die
ripped by war

will they tell us
how ravenous the worms
crawling beneath
our living skin?

will we listen?

How many my lais
atticas
santiagos
will bloat our brains
in silent rage?

many of our friends
are dead
will they tell us of the worms
invading our bones?

We awake to weep,
Allende

They are burning
the breasts of our mother
the earth.

Your sleep within her restless.

And Neruda,
Does that wound in your heart
still hurt?

They fear your words
They burn your words
But your spirit is afire in us.

In our bodies
a terrible thunder
is building its nest.

HOSPITALS ARE TO DIE IN

They finally
had to take obachan
she was dying

      hospitals
      takai
         takai
      she whispered

but she is dying

when they carried her
body
barely breathing,
they were carrying my soul
wrapped in the thin sheath
of her skin.

The ambulance attendants
rushed from their
coffee break
irritated,
dropped her on the
stretcher
and bumped her
against the door
violating her sleep.

She wanted to stay
die in the house
that was like a body
wrapping her
in smells she knew
breathing memories
for her.

In the corners
of her closed eyes
silent tears brimming
protesting
not the hospital

       cold
       white
       expensive

the attendants swore
as they slung
the stretcher

complaining
about the high cost of living.

One said
he had to buy a
side of beef
to hang in his freezer.

       it's cheaper that way.

The desert place. The child knew no other home.

The tortoise crawls in the hot sun. The special sun, like imprisoned, never seeming to move over the flat, flat land. Darkness falls suddenly like a velvet cloth. With it the cold, when the tortoise sleeps.

The child ran barefoot all the time, digging her toes deep into the sand, like a clawed reptile. Unlike them, she could not go beyond the barbed wire.

> Sleep,
> her mother sang,
> the sun will sap
> blood through your pores
> and make you weak.
> Sleep
> in the desert.

When the soldiers came each day, jaws like iron, picking up the men to take them to distant potato fields, she would run after her grandfather, sitting in the back of the army truck with the others, silent. Teeth gripped. Swallowing rage. Her small legs barely would reach the gate as the truck disappeared through the dust.

> Rebellion
> waits outside the gate,
> slowly gathering
> like sounds of angry snowgeese
> or water from the mountain
> springing free.
> Ocean's throat
> calls the awakening.

The children found the tortoise, big, dull shelled, making a slow journey through the desert. They named it Muhon-nin because it would not retreat into its shell, put it in the garden the men had grown from stones and succulents. Making beauty from adversity.

Old men would carve from dead wood in the shade of barracks, resurrecting images of fierce gods. Women made feasts from rations to feed strength. Weaving songs with hidden messages.

<table>
<tr><td>Nenneko, nenneko ya</td><td>sleep, little one</td></tr>
<tr><td>nashite naku yara</td><td>why do you cry?</td></tr>
</table>

Let the tortoise go, the women would say. It is wrong to imprison any living thing.

<table>
<tr><td>Kodomo ga</td><td>children</td></tr>
<tr><td>nemutte iru</td><td>sleeping</td></tr>
<tr><td></td><td>frozen time</td></tr>
<tr><td></td><td>entombs the race</td></tr>
<tr><td></td><td>when will we wake?</td></tr>
</table>

The child, always digging, stepped deep onto a nail. Blood pouring from the bottom of her body. Mother in fear, whispering . . . For those who do not feign sleep, a strange life will follow. Turmoil threatens. Freedom's still a distant harvest.

The tortoise escaped. The children wept.

<table>
<tr><td>Kame kame</td><td>Tortoise takes</td></tr>
<tr><td>nigeru wa</td><td>each step</td></tr>
<tr><td></td><td>inevitable as time</td></tr>
<tr><td></td><td>full with spawn,</td></tr>
<tr><td></td><td>a new age</td></tr>
<tr><td></td><td>to the shore</td></tr>
<tr><td></td><td>where it will bury eggs.</td></tr>
</table>

Her mother washed her feet each day. The child slept, knowing she would run under another sky.

Born in the desert
cord knotted to woman/belly
by barbed wire.
Womb blazing
Beyond bondage.
The sun spreads
in the sand
touching the lip
of the sea,
rising.

The men kept their war inside. Pulling weeds by roots. Figures bent, not broken, wind rounding their backs. Grandfather wears his wait like a shell. Sleep in the desert, he warned.

> Tortoise, empty,
> worn,
> plunges to the deep.
> In the steady
> pounding of the waves,
> offsprings wake.

Mother steady singing by the crib.

> Sleep in the desert.
> Awake in the river.

SHEDDING SILENCE

For Cecil

and four generations of women:

my daughter, Tianne
my mother, Shigemi
and my grandmother, Ichi Inouye

WITHOUT TONGUE

WITHOUT TONGUE

The sun stood among corn, dead in summer.
Dust whirlwinding off dry fields.
He had awoken her for the last time,
burying his head into her shoulder, clawing
open her thighs like the wide branches of stone pine.
She lay, passive, as always. Breathless. Without tongue,
a dead boat on the bottom of the sea,
a wingless beetle waiting for descending shoe.
She dresses. Walks to the meadow shaded
with hawthorne, oak, white birch.
She lifts the rock where she had buried the knife,
afraid she would use it to kill her father.
Her tongue tastes its cold steel edge,
shrill like blood.
She returns to her kitchen, water steaming
in the kettle. Prepares tea
with leaves of shiso no ha, soaked in kyoto plum
and salt. Dried. Sweet bitterness on her tongue.
Chinese flowers bloom in her throat.
She cleans the blade and returns it to the drawer.

JADE JUNKIES

They called her Mamasan Kiru.
She could do anything with a knife.
Gut shrimp
with a single slice
dice
an onion before a tear
could slide.
Make cucumber history
each stroke quick
like a blink
thinner than your skin.
Her knuckles
were scarred from so many
knicks.
Some say she was cut deep
when her G.I. split
and left her
in the middle of America.
She couldn't go back home
in disgrace
so she carved out a place,
her one counter cafe
long before sushi
became fashionable
to jade junkies.
She'd dip her fingers
in ginger sauce
leave her scent
in raw bits of flesh
to make them crave
her flavor.
She'd slip fish
from scale to skin
before blood could think
to surface.

Yea, they'd stand in line
to see her magic
with a knife
scale,   skin
   slice
dice,
   chop.

And they'd always ask,
Do you orientals
do everything
so neatly?

PRISONS OF SILENCE

*(Performed by the Asian American Dance Collective,
1983 Repertory Concert)*

1.
The strongest prisons are built
with walls of silence.

2.
Morning light falls between us
like a wall.
We have laid beside each other
as we have for years.
Before the war, when life
would clamor through our windows,
we woke joyfully to the work.

I keep those moments
like a living silent seed.

After day's work, I would
smell the damp soil in his hands,
his hands that felt the outlines
of my body in the velvet
night of summers.

I hold his warm hands to this
cold wall of flesh
as I have for years.

3.
    Jap!
    Filthy Jap!

    Who lives within me?

    Abandoned homes, confiscated land,
    loyalty oaths, barbed wire prisons
    in a strange wasteland.

Go home, Jap!
Where is home?

A country of betrayal.
No one speaks to us.

We would not speak to each other.

We were accused.

Hands in our hair,
hands that spread our legs
and searched our thighs for secret weapons,
hands that knit barbed wire
to cripple our flight.

Giant hot hands flung me,
fluttering, speechless into
barbed wire, thorns in a broken wing.

The strongest prisons are built
with walls of silence.

4.
I watched him depart that day
from the tedious wall of wire,
the humps of barracks,
handsome in his uniform.

I would look each day for letters
from a wall of time,
waiting for approach of my deliverance
from a wall of dust.

I do not remember
reading about his death
only the wall of wind
that encased me, as I turned my head.

5.

　　U.S. Japs hailed as heroes!

　　I do not know the face of this country
　　it is inhabited by strangers
　　who call me obscene names.

　　Jap. Go home.
　　Where is home?

　　I am alone wandering
　　in this desert.

　　Where is home?
　　Who lives within me?

　　A stranger with knife in her tongue
　　and broken wing,
　　mad from separations and losses cruel
　　as hunger.

　　Walls suffocate her as a tomb,
　　encasing history.

6.

I have kept myself contained
within these wails shaped to my body
and buried my rage.

I rebuilt my life
like a wall, unquestioning.
Obeyed their laws . . . their laws.

7.

　　All persons of Japanese ancestry
　　　　filthy jap
　　Both alien and non-alien
　　　　japs are enemy aliens.
　　To be incarcerated
　　　　for their own good

A military necessity
   The army to handle only the japs.
Where is home?
A country of betrayal.

8.
This wall of silence crumbles
from the bigness of their crimes.
This silent wall
crushed by living memory.

He awakens from the tomb
I have made for myself
and unearths my rage.

I must speak.

9.
He faces me in this small
room of myself.
I find the windows
where light escapes.

From this cell of history
this mute grave,
we birth our rage.

We heal our tongues.

We listen to ourselves

   Korematsu, Hirabayashi, Yasui.

We ignite the syllables of our names.

We give testimony.

We hear the bigness of our sounds freed
like many clapping hands,
thundering for reparations.

We give testimony.

Our noise is dangerous.

10.
We beat our hands
like wings healed.

We soar
from these walls of silence.

GENERATIONS OF WOMEN

I.

      She rests,
rocking to ritual,
the same sun fades
the same blue dress
covering her knees
turned inward
from weariness.
The day is like the work
she shoulders,
sacks of meal, corn, barley.
But her sorrow wears
like steady rain.
She buried him yesterday.
Incense still gathered
in her knuckles knotted
from the rubbings
the massage with nameless
oils, on his swollen gouted feet,
his steel girded back,
muscled from carrying calves,
turning brutal rock,
building fields of promises,
gardens alive with camellias,
peaches, clover.

> *Time has sucked my body.*
> *He is buried*
> *in his one black suit*
> *we kept in mothballs*
> *for that day*
> *I want to lie next to him*
> *in my goldthreaded wedding*
> *kimono, grandly purple*
> *with white cranes in flight,*
> *drape my bones with*
> *wisteria.*

I want to shed the century
of incense resting in my pores
like sweat of dirt.
I want to fly with the birds
in this eternal silk,
heading sunward
for warm matings.
I want this soil
that wraps him
to sleep in the smell
of my work.

    Obachan
walked to the store
wearing respectable
shoes, leather
hard like a wall
against her sole.
She carefully fingered her coins
in the pocket of her thinning
blue dress,
saved for sugar, salt and yellow onions.
The clerk's single syllable spit
out a white wall—
JAP.
She turned to the door
with shopping bag empty as the sound
of her feet in
respectable shoes.
There are no tears
for moments as these.

II.

    Her body speaks,
arms long,
thin as a mantis.

        I am afraid
        to leave this room

of myself, imprisoned
by walls of cloth.
Only the man clocks
my moments,
as he fingers the
corners of my fabric,
empty buttonholes,
my muslin,
sandy as a desert.
I wait.
I wait for his presence,
my flesh like
sheets drying in the wind.
I wait,
weaving chains of flowers
to scent my hands,
color my skin,
mourn my loss.
I wait
for him to open
the bloom
hidden in the folds
of flannel.
I do not remember
being beautiful or proud.

Some losses
can't be counted:
departures to desert camps
and barracks,
men leaving to separate
camps or wars
and finally to houses
walled white full with women
in silk dresses,
wilted flowers and rhinestones
around their necks,
fast drinking, quick joking
women with red lipstick
sleek
and slippery as satin.

Her thin arms
chained by wringing
and worry
and barbed wire
slashing her youth,
her neck bowed to history
and past pain that haunts
her like a slain woman-child.

> *I watched as they*
> *let her die—seventh sister*
> *born like a blue fish into*
> *that dry orange day.*
> *No more women, they prayed,*
> *a son. A son to carry on the name.*

Some losses can't be counted:
abandonments left her
frightened, hungry,
made her count the grains
of rice,
wrinkles in her cheek,
pieces of rock in the desert
sand, shadows of guardtower
soldiers, mornings without
waking men,
the syllables of her name.
Some imprisonments are permanent:
white walls encaged her
with a single syllable:
JAP.
Her lips puckered
from humiliations
that made her feel like mildewed cloth,
smelling with neglect.
Her body a room
helpless to the exit of men.
The day he left her for the
red-lipped woman,
she, damp, wringing,

stood between desert camps
and bedrooms,
brooding for unburied female infants,
her thin arms dripping chains
of flowers
weighted with tears.

III.

Two generations
spit me out
like phlegm,
uncooked rice
one syllable words,
a woman foetus.
There are few places
that are mine.
I claim them,
this ground,
this silent piece of sky
where embroidered cranes keep vigil,
this purple silk smelling of mothballs,
this open cage,
this broken wood from Tule Lake.
I keep these like a rock
in my shoe
to remind me not to weep,
to mend my own body,
to wait not for the entry of men
or ghosts.
I claim
my place
in this line of
generations of women,
lean with work,
soft as tea,
open as the tunnels of the sea
driven as the heels of freedom's feet.
Taut fisted with reparations.

Mother, grandmother
speak in me.
I claim their strong fingers
of patience, their knees
bruised with humiliation,
their hurt, longing,
the sinews of their survival.
Generations of yellow women
gather in me
to crush the white wall
not with the wearing of sorrow
not with the mildew of waiting,
not with brooding or bitterness or regret,
not with wilted flowers or red lipstick.
We crush
the white wall
with a word, a glance,
a garden new with nimosa bamboo,
juniper with barbed wire at their root,
splinters from barracks.
We will come like autumn shedding sleep
a sky about to open with rage,
thunder on high rocks.
I crush
the white wall
with my name.

> *Pronounce it correctly*
> *I say*
> *Curl it on their tongue*
> *Feel each and many*
> *syllable of it,*
> *like grains of warm rice*
> *and that will be pleasing.*

Generations of women
spilling each syllable
with a loud, yellow noise.

DOREEN

Doreen had a round face.
She tried to change it.
Everybody made fun
of her in school.

Her eyes so narrow
they asked if she could see,
called her moonface and
slits.

Doreen frost tipped her hair
ratted it five inches high,
painted her eyes round,
glittering blue shadow up to her brow.

Made her look sad
even when she smiled.

She cut gym all the time
because the white powder on her neck
and face would streak
when she sweat.

But Doreen had boobs
more than most of us Japanese girls
so she wore tight sweaters
and low cut dresses
even in winter.

She didn't hang
with us,
since she put so much time
into changing her face.

White boys
would snicker when she passed by
and word got around
that Doreen
went all the way,
smoked and drank beer.

She told us
she met a veteran
fresh back from Korea.

Fresh back
his leg
still puckered pink
from landmines.

She told us
it was a kick
to listen to his stories
about how they'd torture
the gooks
hang them from trees
by their feet
grenades
in their crotch
and watch
them sweat.

I asked her
why she didn't dig brothers.

And her eyes
would disappear
laughing
so loud
she couldn't hear herself.

One day,
Doreen riding fast
with her friend
went through the windshield
and tore off
her skin
from scalp to chin.

And we were sad.

Because
no one could remember
Doreen's face.

RECIPE

Round Eyes

Ingredients: scissors, Scotch magic transparent tape,
                    eyeliner—water based, black.
                    Optional: false eyelashes.

Cleanse face thoroughly.

For best results, powder entire face, including eyelids.
    (lighter shades suited to total effect desired)

With scissors, cut magic tape 1/16" wide, 3/4"–1/2" long—
depending on length of eyelid.

Stick firmly onto mid-upper eyelid area.
    (looking down into handmirror facilitates finding
    adequate surface)

If using false eyelashes, affix first on lid, folding any
excess lid over the base of eyelash with glue.

Paint black eyeliner on tape and entire lid.

Do not cry.

AMERICAN GEISHA

1.

There are people
who admire
the aesthetics
of our traditions.

And ask politely,
Where are you from?

Lodi
Minneapolis
Chicago
Gilroy
South Bend
Tule Lake
San Francisco
New York
L.A.

They persist and
ask again.

Compliment
our command of the
English language.

2.

American white actress
plays the role
of white American Geisha

filmed on location
in Japan.

It was sooooo hard
says she
because American women walk

in strides

shaking it baby.

Over there,
no hips, no shaking,
point the toes inward and . . .
don't speak
unless spoken to.

Japanese women,
says she,
don't walk.

They place themselves
like art objects.

3.

Mr. Wong
went to Washington, DC
served on a Commission
for Small Businesses.

Was asked
if he was familiar
with the system of free enterprise?

and how come
he didn't speak
with an accent?

4.

They saw
I was Asian
and offered
to revise the program.

So I could read
my poetry
first.

I wouldn't want to follow
HIM.

He is very articulate.

5.

My daughter
was called
F.O.B.

at the beach

bosomed in her swimsuit.

Shake it baby, does it slide sideways?

6.

Do we say thank you?

when they tell us that they've
visited Japan
Hong Kong
Peking
Bali

Guam
Manila
several times

and it's so quaint
lovely
polite
exotic
hospitable
interesting

And when did we arrive?

Since we speak
English so well.

. . . An Asian American college student was
reported to have jumped to her death from
her dormitory window. Her body was found
two days later under a deep cover of snow.
Her suicide note contained an apology to
her parents for having received less than
a perfect four point grade average . . .

SUICIDE NOTE

How many notes written . . .
ink smeared like birdprints in snow.

not good enough not pretty enough not smart enough
dear mother and father.
I apologize
for disappointing you.
I've worked very hard,
not good enough
harder, perhaps to please you.
If only I were a son, shoulders broad
as the sunset threading through pine,
I would see the light in my mother's
eyes, or the golden pride reflected
in my father's dream
of my wide, male hands worthy of work
and comfort.
I would swagger through life
muscled and bold and assured,
drawing praises to me
like currents in the bed of wind, virile
with confidence.
not good enough not strong enough not good enough

I apologize.
Tasks do not come easily.
Each failure, a glacier.
Each disapproval, a bootprint.

Each disappointment,
ice above my river.
So I have worked hard.
                    not good enough
My sacrifice I will drop
bone by bone, perched
on the ledge of my womanhood,
fragile as wings.
                    not strong enough
It is snowing steadily
surely not good weather
for flying—this sparrow
sillied and dizzied by the wind
on the edge.
                    not smart enough
I make this ledge my altar
to offer penance.
This air will not hold me,
the snow burdens my crippled wings,
my tears drop like bitter cloth
softly into the gutter below.
     not good enough not strong enough not smart enough

                    Choices thin as shaved
                    ice. Notes shredded
                    drift like snow

on my broken body,
covers me like whispers
of sorries
sorries.
Perhaps when they find me
they will bury
my bird bones beneath
a sturdy pine
and scatter my feathers like
unspoken song
over this white and cold and silent
breast of earth.

BREAKING TRADITION

For my daughter

My daughter denies she is like me,
her secretive eyes avoid mine.
    She reveals the hatreds of womanhood
    already veiled behind music and smoke and telephones.
I want to tell her about the empty room
    of myself.
    This room we lock ourselves in
    where whispers live like fungus,
    giggles about small breasts and cellulite,
    where we confine ourselves to jealousies,
    bedridden by menstruation.
    This waiting room where we feel our hands
    are useless, dead speechless clamps
    that need hospitals and forceps and kitchens
    and plugs and ironing boards to make them useful.
I deny I am like my mother.   I remember why:
    She kept her room neat with silence,
    defiance smothered in requirements to be otonashii,
    passion and loudness wrapped in an obi,
    her steps confined to ceremony,
    the weight of her sacrifice she carried like
    a foetus. Guilt passed on in our bones.
I want to break tradition—unlock this room
    where women dress in the dark.
    Discover the lies my mother told me.
    The lies that we are small and powerless
    that our possibilities must be compressed
    to the size of pearls, displayed only as
    passive chokers, charms around our neck.
Break Tradition.
    I want to tell my daughter of this room
    of myself
    filled with tears of shakuhachi,
    the light in my hands,

poems about madness,
the music of yellow guitars,
sounds shaken from barbed wire and
goodbyes and miracles of survival.

My daughter denies she is like me
her secretive eyes are walls of smoke
and music and telephones.
her pouting ruby lips, her skirts
swaying to salsa, Madonna and the Stones.
her thighs displayed in carnavals of color.
I do not know the contents of her room.
She mirrors my aging.

She is breaking tradition.

SHADOW IN STONE

Journey to Hiroshima, Japan
International Peace Conference, 1984

We wander in the stifling heat
of August.
Hiroshima,
your museum, peace park,
paper cranes rustling whispers
of hei-wa   *peace*
Burning incense
throbbing with white chrysanthemums,
plum blossoms, mounds
of soundless bones.
Hiroshima
how you rise up
in relentless waves of heat.
I come to you late,
when the weather bludgeons, blisters.
      I put my mouth
on your burning sky
on the lips of your murmuring river.
Motoyasu, river of the dead.

      The river speaks:
        I received the bodies
        leaping into my wet arms
        their flesh in flame, and the flies
        that followed
        maggots in the bloated sightless waste,
        skin rotting like wet leaves.
        My rhythm stifled, my movement stilled.

Motoyasu cries with rituals,
bearing a thousand flickering candles
in floating lanterns of yellow, red, blue
to remember the suffering.

I light a lantern for grandmother's sister
whom they never found amidst the ashes
of your cremation.
She floats beside the other souls
as we gather, filling water
in the cups of our hands,
pouring it back into the thirsty mouths
of ghosts, stretching parched throats.

The heat presses like many hands.
I seek solace in the stone
with human shadow burned into its face.
         I want to put my mouth to it
to the shoulders of that body,
my tongue to wet its dusty heart.

         I ask the stone to speak:
                  When I looked up,
                  I did not see the sun
                  a kind friend who has gently pulled
                  my rice plants skyward.
                  I worried in that moment
                  if my child would find shade
                  in this unbearable heat
                  that melts my eyes.
                  No, I did not see the sun.
                  I saw what today
                  mankind has created
                  and I laid my body
                  into this cool stone,
                  my merciful resting place.

Museum of ruins.
The heat wrings our bodies
with its many fingers.
Photographs remind us of a holocaust
and imagination stumbles, beaten, aghast.

I want to put my mouth
against these ruins, the distorted teacup,
crippled iron,
melted coins,
a disfigured bowl.

I ask the bowl to speak:
The old man
held his daughter,
rocking her in his lap,
day after day after
that terrible day,
she weak from radiation
could not lift this bowl.
Her face once bright like our sunset
now white as ash,
could not part her lips
as he tried to spoon okayu from this bowl
droplet by droplet
into the crack of her mouth,
the watered rice with umeboshi
which he would chew to feed her.
He did not know
when she stopped breathing
as he put his mouth to hers
gently to pass food.
He rocked her still body
watching the red sunset
burning its fiery farewell.

Hiroshima, rising up.
I come here late
when the weather sucks at us.
I want to put my mouth
to the air, its many fingers of heat,
lick the twisted lips
of a disfigured bowl,

the burned and dusty heart of shadow in stone,
put my mouth to the tongues
of a river,
its rhythms, its living water
weeping on the sides of lanterns,
each floating flame, a flickering
voice murmuring
over and over
as I put my mouth
to echo
over and over
never again.

After forty years of silence
about the experience of Japanese
Americans in World War II concentration
camps, my mother testified before the
Commission on Wartime Relocation and
Internment of Japanese American
Civilians in 1981.

BREAKING SILENCE

For my mother

There are miracles that happen
she said.
From the silences
in the glass caves of our ears,
from the crippled tongue,
from the mute, wet eyelash,
testimonies waiting like winter.
         We were told
that silence was better
golden like our skin,
         useful like
go quietly,
         easier like
don't make waves,
         expedient like
horsestalls and deserts.

                    "Mr. Commissioner . . .
                    . . . the U.S. Army Signal Corps confiscated
                    our property . . . it was subjected to
                    vandalism and ravage. All improvements
                    we had made before our incarceration
                    was stolen or destroyed . . .

———————————————————

(Quoted excerpts from my mother's testimony modified with her permissions)

I was coerced into signing documents
giving you authority to take . . ."
to take
to take.

My mother,
soft as tallow,
words peeling from her
like slivers of yellow flame.
Her testimony,
a vat of boiling water
surging through the coldest
bluest vein.
        She had come to her land
as shovel, hoe and sickle searing
reed and rock and dead brush,
labored to sinew the ground
to soften gardens pregnant with seed
awaiting each silent morning
birthing
fields of flowers,
mustard greens and tomatoes
throbbing like the sea.
        And then
All was hushed for announcements:
        "Take only what you can carry . . ."
We were made to believe our faces
betrayed us.
Our bodies were loud
with yellow screaming flesh
needing to be silenced
behind barbed wire.

        "Mr. Commissioner . . .
        . . . it seems we were singled out
        from others who were under suspicion.
        Our neighbors were of German and

Italian descent, some of whom were
not citizens . . . It seems we were
singled out . . ."

She had worn her work
like lemon leaves,
shining in her sweat,
driven by her dreams that honed
the blade of her plow.
The land she built
like hope
grew quietly
irises, roses, sweet peas
opening, opening.
    And then
all was hushed for announcements:
    ". . . to be incarcerated for your own good"
The sounds of her work
bolted in barracks . . .
silenced.

Mr. Commissioner . . .
So when you tell me I must limit
testimony
when you tell me my time is up,
I tell you this:
Pride has kept my lips
pinned by nails
my rage coffined.
But I exhume my past
to claim this time.
My youth is buried in Rohwer,
Obachan's ghost visits Amache Gate.
My niece haunts Tule Lake.
Words are better than tears,
so I spill them.
I kill this,
the silence . . .

There are miracles that happen
she said,
and everything is made visible.
        We see the cracks and fissures in our soil:
We speak of suicides and intimacies,
of longings lush like wet furrows,
of oceans bearing us toward imagined riches,
of burning humiliations and
crimes by the government.
Of self hate and of love that breaks
through silences.
        We are lightning and justice.
        Our souls become transparent like glass
revealing tears for war-dead sons
red ashes of Hiroshima
jagged wounds from barbed wire.
        We must recognize ourselves at last.
        We are a rainforest of color
and noise.
        We hear everything.
        We are unafraid.

        Our language is beautiful.

TOMATOES

"We have to read The Red Badge of Courage.*"*
   "We all had to read it."
"But all heroes are not men."
            Dialogue with my daughter

Hanako loved her garden. She and her young daughter lived with her parents on a farm planted in the stretch of fields near Gilroy. Her husband died during the war. He was a hero. Received medals and letters of commendation for valor in battle, for defending his country, for saving fellow soldiers in his regiment.

Hanako had delivered to her an American flag and his medal after she and her parents got out of the concentration camp located in the middle of the desert.

When they returned to her parents' farm, the house had to be repaired and rebuilt and the land was dried, cracked like weathered skin.

Hanako would look out over the wide flat expanse of the valley. In the dry season it reminded her of the camp desert where the heat would shimmer up and if you looked long enough you thought you could see someone approaching. She'd do that a lot, dreaming her husband would be running toward her. She'd shade her eyes and watch as the sun pulsated, conjuring up the man with the strong warm hands that would go up her neck and through her hair and pull her face close to him. The heat from the ground would travel through her body and she would weep from the barrenness of knowing he would never be coming back.

Lisa looked like him, his squarish jaw, his deep black eyes, the smile lines in her cheek.

           Mommy, I want red flowers.

Hanako set about to soften her earth, make her garden. She wielded her hoe like a sword, breaking hard crusts of dirt. Lisa would bring out the hose and buckets to help moisten the ground, playing in the water, muddy pools created by Hanako's shovel. She planted bright geraniums that grew sturdily in dry climate next to her tomato vines.

The Haufmanns who lived four acres away came over the day they returned to the farm, talked about the hard times they had during the war and difficulties in keeping up their own land. They just couldn't afford to water anyone else's crops even with the extra money and the furniture, china, tractor, seedlings, livestock they were given by Hanako's parents

before their hasty departure to the camps. Mr. Haufmann kicked the dirt
as he commented that Hanako didn't look any the worse for wear. He
eyed her breasts under her white cotton blouse, and admired how Lisa
had grown into a fine young girl with slender hips like her
mommy and so sorry
to hear about the husband.
    Hanako answered politely
        the war is over and done.
        We've come back to start our life again
        like planting new seeds and hoping they'll
        grow stronger.

    Mr. Haufmann would frequently visit if he'd see Hanako and Lisa in
their resurrected garden, weeding, pulling the dandelion from her tender
tomato vines, her sweet peas with their thin delicate stalks climbing the
stakes she had hammered into the ground in neat rows, the robust thick
stubs of kale, and Lisa's geraniums brightly red in the heat.
        Kinda delicate, aren't you, doing
        all this work? Skin's going to shrivel
        in this mean sun.   Work's too heavy for little girls.
    Hanako would stand up straight and speak politely, softly,
        there are many things we must learn
        to do without
        and find the strength
        to do ourselves.
    Lisa, tending her flowers, ran up to Mr. Haufmann who lifted her high
in the air, her skirt flying above her panties. Mr. Haufmann laughing,
flinging her up again and again, until Hanako would tell Lisa to finish
her watering chores, her eyes turning black and silent as she whacked at
the heads of dandelion weeds with her hoe.
    The heat rose early that day, its fingers clutching the rows of dirt.
Hanako from the kitchen window did not see Lisa in the garden, watering
as she usually did. She went immediately outside, looking, instinctively
picked up her hoe and walked through the shimmering heat.
    Hanako started toward the Haufmann farm when she saw Lisa
running toward her with a paper bag.
        Mommy. Mommy. Mr. Haufmann
        gave me pears and figs. They're ripe
        and sweet. He let me climb and pick

them myself. He's so strong, let me
stand on his shoulders so I could reach
the top branches.
Hanako's knuckles turned white on the handle of the hoe, told Lisa
she was not to play at the Haufmann's again, returned to her garden and
sprayed for insects.

Mr. Haufmann appeared in the waves of heat that afternoon, wiping
off his face with the back of his hand. Hanako's sweat ran down her back,
popped above her mouth. Haufmann redfaced, smiling
Tomatoes looking good and juicy.
Got a lotta nice young buds gonna pop soon, too.
Heat's good for them I guess.
Hanako with her hoe turned the soil gently,
How's your wife? Haven't seen her for awhile.
Wetting his lips
O, that old mare's too tired to
walk even this distance. Just sits at the
radio and knits. Damn knitting gets on
my nerves.
Hanako's hoe, turning, turning
And your sons. Are they doing well?
Haufmann's hard laugh
Too good for farming. Both in college,
and don't hardly write or call. Busy
chasing women and getting into trouble.
Ha. Rascals they are. Men will be men.
Hanako's hoe fiercely cutting near the tomato vines
You are fortunate to have healthy children.
Hanako's hoe high in the air, whacked like a sword through a ripe
tomato, juices springing up, smearing the soil
There's nothing we won't do
to insure their happiness, is there?
her voice low and glinting now like her blade as she whacked off the head
of another tomato smearing the handle red. Haufmann's eyes, fading
lights of blue, blinked as he stepped backward. Hanako's voice now like
the edge of sharp knives almost whispering
We see so much of ourselves
mirrored in our children
except more . . .

Whack. Hanako's hoe now fiercely slicing, thudding, crushing the ripened crop of tomatoes as the blade smeared red, the handle now slippery with juices and pink seeds

> I have no bitterness Mr. Haufmann
>
> not about the war, nor the losses.

She thought of her husband's final moments.
Did he suffer long. What were his thoughts . . .

> the humiliation of those camps.

Did he remember her and their chubby Lisa waving
from the wire fence as he left them for the war?

> the work or this heat
>
> or the loneliness.
>
> Only the regret
>
> that my husband

The memory of smile lines in his cheek,
his warm hands stroking Lisa's hair,
quieting her in his rocking arms,

> cannot see the growing,
>
> budding living hope

Lisa came running to her mother's side, speechless at the devastation, the red mass of crushed tomatoes, her eyes wide and instantly older, seeing Haufmann wilting
shriveled in sweat and the wrinkles
of his wet shirt.
He, wordless, slumped
to escape
into the waves of heat.

> Mother. I'm so glad
>
> you saved my geraniums.

I have seen you

    when the delta floods,
    packing mud,
    sandbags, protecting
    the fields like your woman.

    in the trees
    when the oranges
    were ripe,
    filling your hands

    in strawberry patches
    warming buds
    against the frost
    with your breath.

    in a slow dance
    eyes closed
    remembering the tall grasses
    near your village
    whispering your name.

I have seen your sons

    eyes flaring
    in halls of injustice,
    commission rooms
    spewing yellow rage.

in the lot on Kearny
that yawns like a grave,
kicking the remains
he tried to save.

with shaking hands,
too gentle for words
on the shoulders
of our grandmothers.

I have seen you

    scooping rice and cha
    steamed fish, pansit,
    snow peas and pak-kai
    tsukemono
    into your laughing mouth.

My brothers,
I have seen you.

My eyes blur
sometimes

at beauty.

SLAYING DRAGON LADIES

On seeing the movie
"The Year of the Dragon"

My fingernails
are long, steel tipped,
sharp as stilettos
to more easily pluck
your eyes,
cleanly sever it from its nerve,
roll it in my palm.
We believe the eye
brings luck, health.
Seasoned with shoyu,
sucked like embryos from eggs.
Ahhh. the nourishment.
My epicanthic fold
lined in red
is the sister of the tiger.
My tongue will moisten
you for easier
swallowing.
Eat your eyes
while I ride you,
my cunt a moving mouth.
Female dragons are born there.
        You don't know me.
        Madame Nhu,
        Anna Chenault,
        Imelda Marcos are not reputed
        for their compassion, after all.
Or you may prefer
my smell to be lush
as damp forests,
exotic as flowered trees.
I dwell in a house of bamboo,
kneeling to the sound of reed flute.
My small hands
folded obediently in my lap.

I wait to serve you
tea,
shuffle to you in
plum scented kimono
on my knees,
speak in whispers
when spoken to and bow
to your growing
fantasy.
      You don't know me.
      Geisha girl.
      China Doll.
      Slant cunt whore.
      Objects dangled
      in the glare.

The sun meets a place
in the sky
and there are no shadows.
You cannot see me.
      my breasts are Manzanar's desert
      my thighs an Arkansas swamp
      my veins are California's railroads
      my feet a Chicago postwar ghetto.
I prepare slowly
with the memory
of my mother who is
civilized,
my father who
fought a war for you,
my grandmother, compassionate,
who forgave you.
My hands are steady.
Pentipped fingers
drenched in ink.
Ready for the slaying.

      You will know me.

IT ISN'T EASY

IT ISN'T EASY

For Cecil

I want to give you
everything
yet nothing . . .
    my silence
a cup of tea,
chatter . . .
    the ants
invading our cannisters,
dishes piled like angry words,
dust gathering in corners
like unswept thought . . .
    It would be easier
this smallness of giving,
this reduction to detail
of maintenance:
the attention to
stockings that need mending,
the filling up of holes,
the knitting of emptiness.
    It would be easier
to be your victim.
Seduced by complacency
effortless acquiescence.
Let you pilot my passive
body into unknown ports . . .
abdicate to the whirling air
of your arms, and unresisting,
be tossed into the haunches of midnight.
    I want to give you
nothing,
yet everything:
the dreams I navigate
lapping on the shores of
Honshu to the Ivory Coast,
the hibiscus blooming
between my thighs,

        my poems
strung like bloody beads across my throat,
my disembowelment, my seppuku—
scarlet entrails
twisting from the open wound,
        my dark words
unbridled like horses
steaming nostrils, hoof, mane.

        It isn't easy
to bring to your hands
a storm of bloodred flowers
and brutal birthings,
        not easy
this passion for power, my unbeautiful hunger,
this selfish desire to be loud, bigger
than light, this longing
for movement, my own,
this discovery of unveiled women
rising up,
and tongueless ones
rising up . . .
        this rising up
through empty sockholes,
teacups, dishes, antfilled cannisters,
dust and acquiescence.
        It isn't easy
this love rising up
beside your great expanse.
Each lifting its own air,
yellow
dark
feathered flight,
filling the sky
with color and strange song.
A dazzle of independence.

It isn't easy.

IN REMEMBRANCE

For Uncle Minoru, Died January, 1984

We gather at your coffin,
Uncle Minoru.
Mother, with her hands like gardenias
touches your sleeves.
We whisper of how well you look
peaceful in your utter silence.
How much we remember.
Why now, at death?
      Your kindnesses, Uncle,
as you crafted paper monkeys,
multicolored birds
to climb and jerk on a stick
to amuse children who gathered
at your innocent dark eyes,
always slightly moist.
We would jump on your back, riding you
like a silent horse,
as you lumbered on your hands and knees
from room to room.
      How much we remember . . .
we rode your shoulders,
knotted with hurt,
dressed in faded denim, smelling like
laundry soap and fish.
You never complained of it
only through those dark moist eyes.
And your smile
that drew living animals to you,
even wild birds.
Obachan said they could smell
the wounds hiding in your throat,
the wound in your heart
pierced by unjust punishment, racism, and rejection
sharp as blades.

When did you vow silence, Minoru?
After the camps,
after you buried a daughter?
You slumped into a light
of your own and let life ride you.
Your daughter thrown broken
on the road by a drunk driver
who mumbled she flew from nowhere like a dumb chicken,
stretched out $200, not one apology
and said we were safer in the camps.

Was there nothing left to say, Minoru,
as you slapped away his hot white hand?

How much we remember . . .
When they took you to Amache Gate
locked us up like herded horses,
your dark innocent eyes, moist
with disbelief at charges of
sabotage, espionage,
your shoulders staggered from the lies.
Fear like a cold finger
pressed at your heart.
Life gasped like a beached fish.
The sky scummed over with clouds
and punishment without crime
stabbed between the blades of your back.

Was there nothing left to say?
Minoru, the children who rode you
have tongues like birds.
We chatter. We remember
the mounds of hurt at your shoulders.
Could we but massage them to soothe
the pain, but death
makes our regrets scattered as apologies.
We did not expect them
to rip the coat of pride from your bones
nor the melody from your throat.

Yes, there is much to say.
We will not leave your memory
as a silent rancid rose.

Our tongues become livid with history and
demands for reparations.
Crimes are revealed like the bloody lashes
of a fallen whip:
>the falsehoods, deletions, the conspiracy
>to legalize mass imprisonment.
No, we will not forget
>Amache Gate, Rohwer, Poston, Heart Mountain,
>Minidoka, Jerome, Gila River, Manzanar,
>Topaz, Tule Lake.
Our tongues are sharp like blades,
we overturn furrows of secrecy.
>Yes, we will harvest justice.
And Uncle, perhaps
your spirit will return
alive in a horse, or a bird,
riding free in the wind,
life surging through
the sinews of your strong shoulders.
>And yes,
the struggle continues on
with our stampede of voices.

SOUL FOOD

For Cecil

We prepare
the meal together.
I complain,
hurt, reduced to fury
again by their
subtle insults
insinuations
because I am married to you.
Impossible autonomy, no mind
of my own.

You like your fish
crisp, coated with cornmeal,
fried deep,
sliced mangos to sweeten
the tang of lemons.
My fish is raw,
on shredded lettuce,
lemon slices thin as skin,
wasabe burning like green fire.
You bake the cornbread flat
and dip it in
the thick soup
I've brewed from
turkey carcass, rice gruel,
sesame oil and chervil.

We laugh over watermelon
and bubbling cobbler.

You say,
there are few men
who can stand
to have a woman equal,
upright.

This meal,
Unsurpassed.

SPOILS OF WAR

Violet ran up the familiar path of Telman Park determined today to make five miles. She knew the exact spot of her destination, through the eucalyptus, past the emergency telephone box, up to the twin boulders where she would sit triumphantly and rest in the warm sun.

He watched her from his green Volkswagen van. Her black hair bouncing at her shoulder blades, her sturdy thighs and sleek runner's calves. Her small breasts jousled with each step under the sweatshirt that read, "Lotus Blossom Doesn't Live Here."

> Spirit of the bayonet.
> red/harch
> white/hup
> blue/eyes front
> square your piece
> left/right
> kill 'em
> thrust/jab
> jab
> jab/kill 'em.
> "hey mamasan,
> joto mate ichiban"
> poontang one/two
> poontang three/four
> when we're done
> we'll kill some more.

Of all the joggers he saw, this was the one he wanted. He would park and watch the several who, at the same time each day, would run the path up into the wooded hills of the park.

Violet started running after she had met Josh. In fact, she started doing a lot of things. All her life she had been introverted, studious, conscientious, shy. During her last graduate year, life revolted around her. There were so many demonstrations on campus against the Vietnam war, she didn't pay attention to the noises—the speeches, doomsday messages from wild-eyed street preachers and twitching panhandlers. So when the police stormed the gathered protestors, Violet did not move out of the way in time as the sweep of billyclubs and helmets picked her up like a wave. Violet hit the cement with her elbow and curled up reflexively to protect her head from the stampede of legs and feet. Josh had stumbled over her and scrambling up, lifted her with him.

In the months of their new friendship, the world she had pulled around herself like a narrow corridor began to swell and pulse as they talked of civil rights, the war, military tycoonism, racism that had many faces. They saw and touched their common wounds.

Josh talked about his war. He who escaped the draft, his mother's endless work to help him through college, his father whose heart was crushed by the humiliation of worklessness. His father's death gave him life, the circumstance for exemption from the military, and the freedom to revolt, protest.

Violet talked about her war. The sheets of silence that covered history from the moment the gates slammed her parents into concentration camps in Arkansas. Her mother distant and forgetful. Her father demanding, critical. It didn't seem to matter what Violet achieved. They kept their silence like blades beneath their tongues.

Violet passed the old eucalyptus, branching high, its constant falling leaves and shedding bark making the air smell pungent. She noticed the green van, dismissed it in the glaring light of afternoon.

He crouched lower behind the wheel as she passed, seeing her closer, the dark sloping eyes, her olive skin browned by the sun, her delicate mouth and bones above her cheek. The beads of sweat popping around her brow.

> They all had Vietnamese women.
> None like mine.
> She was bamboo thin,
> her fingers clutching
> the hem of her sleeve
> like a child.
> I felt red flame
> licking the nape of my neck burning
> deeper than napalm.
> She was quiet,
> her eyes, darker than night
> helped me forget my My Lais.

Her beautiful body
curling around me,
flesh cocooned me against the
jungle where eyes were like rain.
Her arms like ivory bracelets
encircling my pain.
Flesh whole, sensual, shining
amidst the stench of rotting wounds
that fed the fat flies.
The insatiable flies of Vietnam.

Violet felt her anger draining with each step. The pounds shed, the tightening of her thighs, the new curves at her hips, and the thoughts of leaving home soon. Free as the wind in her face. Free from the jagged silences of her mother, the brooding disapproval of her father. Violet had informed them that she would be moving in with Josh. Perhaps they would live in Oregon where he was interviewing for a job at the University. She smiled, thinking of Josh's return, his sardonic grin when she told him of her parents' reaction. Josh who encouraged her to run, to strengthen herself, to speak her mind, to open her body, so long wrapped in years of suffocation. Her body that she had felt pitifully shapeless, small, powerless, burdened with blame and fault. If only he had not died. He was not due for another month. Her mother's face, pinched in pain as water and blood ran from her, rushed to the hospital. Her mother's body, wracked, gray, heaving and bellowing. The child tearing to exit too soon. She could still hear the screams from her mother's bones. The son, born dead. She remembered feeling alone. The weight of their grief, the sense of regret that she remained alive, on her small shoulders. All these years, the weight like boulders, the weight now shedding with each step.

The sun was a hot hand on her back as Violet ran through the threaded leaves, cracking beneath her steady feet.

He could feel the drugs wearing off. His skin twitching. He imagined the sores popping anew, the smell from jungle rot seeping from his pale flesh, tinted blue. He knew he would vomit.

She never withheld her warm thighs,
even when gorged with woman blood,
hot blood
sucking me deeper into her.
All the blood that would fill
a river.

Those jungles, villages like
a body split, slit, gouged.
Blood on me.
Swelling within her,
my blade, gleaming in the moonlight
exits flesh, flashes in her eyes.
She licks the blood from the shaft.
Deep, I thrust it past her teeth.
She took it all
her throat tightening on it
blood bubbling from the edges
of her lips.
Her arms circling my hips,
her hands moving in my groin
with grenade.
My blade cuts the arm away,
splits her womb
that spumes hot blood.

Violet noticed the day emptier, the sun hotter. No wind. She would reach her boulders today. Her mouth open slightly as she pushed her breath. The path became clearer, the trees very still. Like entering a strange new place. She remembered her corridor where she withdrew, compressed by whispers of guilt, mother's unhappiness, father's loneliness. Her narrow corridor, airless. Dark. Her flesh lined the walls. Josh's hands touching, warming her surfaces, expanding. His long runner's body entering her corners. Breathing. She discovers sensation. Muscles moving, sinews of desire. Nerve endings alive.

Violet stood before her parents and shouted. Her mother threatened to kill herself. Her father informed her she could never bring Josh into his house. It was bad enough to marry outside her race, but to live in sin with someone especially *that* color is endless disgrace. Violet's fury unleashed like exploding walls. She would leave this week. Run free of them. Lift it all from her like the wind picking up leaves and spinning them to the sky.

The son, blue and breathless, wrinkled like a raisin. Mother gave up back then, switched off her eyes. Her dull face all these years never saw her daughter's pain. Well, Violet didn't want to take it on anymore. Can't bring him back to life. Can't trade places, can't be what they want, no matter what she did. Had he lived, he'd be in college or a soldier drafted, maybe dead anyway in Southeast Asia.

Violet running faster. She'd live her own life. She could see the boulders now.

He, crouching behind the trees, watched her lengthening shadow climbing the boulder where she lay down, stretched her bare arms and legs glistening with sweat. Her body lifted by her panting breath.

He pulls her by both legs onto the ground. She is surprised. not knowing how she fell. He pulls her to him, hand over her mouth and drags her into the trees. Her legs are strong, digging into the soft earth, resisting, thrashing. He reveals the long knife unsheathed, whispers that he will cut her throat if she screams. Violet retreats into her corridor, breathing quietly through her nose. He leads her far from the path, under brush and thicket of trees. He commands her to kneel in the leaves. Violet, terror exploding, screams, her fists beating against his pressing body, suffocating, scarred, distorted flesh. He falls upon her like a rock. His fists beat her again, brutally again, until she is unconscious. He pulls her shorts off, and gently. Gently. Caressing, kisses her slightly open mouth, her neck, her still arms. Inserts his blade in her womb and makes her bleed.

After, he carefully dresses himself. With a wide arched swing of his sharp knife, he severs her arm above the elbow.

Wiping the blood from his blade, gently he wraps the arm in his flak jacket. Carries it like a child to his van and leaves.

The wind is still, the sun falling, casting long shadows from the boulders, the trees. In the thicket, the faint hum of flies gathering.

> Spirit of the bayonet.
> red/harch
> white/hup
> blue/eyes front
> Square your piece
> left/right
> kill 'em
> thrust/jab
> jab
> jab/kill 'em
> "hey mamasan
> joto mate ichiban"
> poontang one/two
> poontang three/four
> when we're done
> we'll kill some more.

HEALTHY CHOICES

Hold still

Keep quiet.

Get a degree
to learn how to talk
saying nothing.

Catch a good man
by being demure.
the one your mother chooses.

Let him climb you
whenever his urge,
amidst headaches
and menstrual aches
and screaming infants.
And when he bids
quick, turn over.

Hold still.

Make your tongue
a slab of cement
a white stone etched
with your name.
Kill your stories with knives
and knitting needles
and Clorox bleach.

Hide in your mysteriousness
by saying nothing.

Starch your thoughts
with ironed shirts.

Tie your anger
with a knot in
your throat
and when he comes
without concern,
swallow it.

Hold still.

Keep desire
hopeless as ice
and sleepless nights
and painful as a pinched eyelid.

Keep your fingers
from the razor,
keep your longing
to sever
his condescension
safely in your douchbag.

Turn the blade
against yourself.
Don't twitch
as your slashed wrists
stain your bathroom tiles.
Disinfect with Pine Sol.

Hold still.

Keep quiet.

Keep tight your lips,
keep dead your dreams,
keep cold your heart.

Keep quiet.

And he will shout
praises
to your
perfection.

THE LOVERS

The man came
in from the field.
He said nothing
to the woman
and began to eat
that which she prepared for him.
They moved,
carefully
inevitably
as the silent keeping
of time.

For them,
it moved nowhere
but to etch lines
on the woman's face,
the man's hands.
"The plums are small"
is all he said.
The woman,
facing the man,
speechless,
poured the steaming tea
slowly to half cup.
  (The steam,
  ghosting her vision,
  her desire
  her unspoken words:)

    I will start with your
    hands,
    and slowly
    with the sickle

slice the folds
of each finger
so blood will
form patterns
like the scales of fish.
Then I will hold the slivers
of flesh
and peel them slowly
as we do the skin of ripe
plums
until your eyes
widen with the pain
until the bone
appears like hope.
You will wince
as I approach
your face
with my razor sharp
fish knife
and carve your cheekbones
leaving only the flesh
around your eyebrows
shaped like wings.
And your eyes,
that are indifferent like the dead
will come alive
with horror/seeing me
for the first time.

Listen, listen
I will whisper
to the rhythm of your blood
rippling like the river
that feeds your plums.

The man gazes up
at her,
        (she is straddling him
        with the blade between her teeth
        a love never seen before
        in his smile)
he does not smile.
        (and he will say:)

                I hear the singing of plums
                drinking the earth,
                sucking the sun.
                You have kept your breasts
                hidden from me
                in darkness.
                I could only feel
                the ripe smooth bursting
                as I entered
                the root place
                between your thighs.
                Silence has been my defense
                of your woman masterhood.

                The trees are my friends.
                What they ask of me,
                I can give.
                What I plant
                I get back.
                What I nourish
                I eat.
                Entering the house
                with you in your silent
                making
                your suffocating
                servitude,
                I will pull with my strong neck
                the plow blade,

you, like the shaft of wheat
slipping to the threshing
floor
scattered there like seed.
I will run the blade
first up the sides
of your thighs
until your blood
has grained the wood.

The woman, wordless,
pours his tea
silently.

The man,
eyes indifferent like the dead
says,
"The plums are small
this year."

FATS

I should've gotten mad.

I must be getting old.

Children
waste like cornflakes
in a milkless tenderloin room,
carried off by
rats
that are everywhere,
getting fat.

Fats got himself stuck
in the plumbing.
Died. Decaying.
Water running through
his corpse.

Pregnant women drink,
children wet their cornflakes.

I get sick.

I must be getting old.

WHAT MATTERS

WHAT MATTERS

The things that matter
you ask, where is love?
The poem
soft as linen
dried by the sun?
words of comfort
like puffed pillows
yellow flowers
with velvet petals?
Where is serenity,
cherry blossoms arranged,
the quaint ceremony of tea?
Images metaphysically deep
spoken in Japanese,
preferably seventeen syllables
of
persimmons or new
plums or snow covered bridges
or red flow of leaves?
What matters
the trickling clarity of
water
each day, not fearing thirst.
        I love you
when persimmons sweat
shining in a sand gray bowl,
        Mama
hiding pennies
under floor boards
with flour, saltine crackers,
balls of used aluminum foil,
string, coupons and water jars
secreted for that day.

That day
when all would be taken
and packing
must be quick again.
      I love you
when snow covers the bridge
curved over ice white water
          Grandfather
killing my cat
who ripped open his hens,
sucking their eggs.
His eyes, half closed
behind steel rims,
cigarette holder
clenched in his teeth,
as he fondled the rock.
Before I could cry
or plead,
my cat, writhing
with skull crushed.
He captured a rabbit,
gave it to me
and warned
we would eat in winter
as soon as I began to love her.

      I love you
when plums burst like new moons,
crescents on their black boughs
        my husband
whose dark hands
embrace the wilted shoulders
of the wretched,
winos with wracked eyes,
and welfare mothers cleaning cockroaches
from the lips of their children.
His words
like spoons, nourishing.

I love you
when leaves flow in crimson,
orange, yellow, sepia waves
        my daughter
who weeps for each dead
seal, murdered tiger,
cat's corpse, endangered species
of condor and Chinese panda,
crusading against gamesmen
and trophy hunters.
        What matters,
Breath
for the shipwrecked, drowning.
        What matters
amidst the dread of nuclear winter,
Chernobyl's catastrophe, Three Mile Island,
Nevada's test veterans, terrorism,
the massacred in Port Elizabeth, the
wounded of Central America, genocide of drugs,
AIDS, toxic waste, Atlanta's missing
and mutilated, hunger, mistaken identities,
murder in the streets.
        A love poem?

        Clear water passing   (5)
        our mouths unafraid to breathe,   (7)
        and to speak freely.   (5)

GRACIELLA

Graciella's arms,
big like hammocks
swaying mounds of work,
her eyes like moons
moving the waves
of soil   breaking
bursting green leaves
iceberg lettuce.

        and he watched
        from the shade of his elm,
        pleased.

From her body
glistened
wires of water across
her face,
her big arms
cradled the work,
her hands like a weaver,
threading the dirt
to a rich, dark rug
until the sun fell
behind the elm.

        best damned worker
        I ever had,
        good as a dozen wetbacks
        even with the kid
        strapped
        to her back he said, pleased.

From her body
she pushed a child
head swollen
veins rippling
from his hairless skull

        no work, no pay
        she doesn't miss a day
        they push 'em out like rabbits
        he said, pleased.

Into her body
she sucked the sun,
the soil, into her fingers
her pores,
into her nostrils,
her throat
the white chemical dust
sprayed from the cropduster
into her blood
that ran through her child
who died writhing like a hooked worm.

She did not work
that day.

        Displeased,
        he docked her pay.

        He did not offer
        her child's grave
        to be planted in the shade
        of his elm.

ASSAULTS AND INVASIONS

Linette was beaten daily.
He said she wasn't any good, dumb and weak even for a woman.

Every time I'd see her, face swollen like a bruised soft peach, lip hanging big and purple over her chin, her eyes bled hunger and helplessness. When he would start in on her, she could only defend with fingernails and sweat and a tongue fat with broken veins and angry words. She is a hundred and five pounds powerless to his two hundred pound body, and she opens her legs like murdered wheat. She moved out several times, this time reporting him to the police, begged the courts to restrain him. He found her, and when she wouldn't whimper or cry or open her thighs this time, he with his razor began to slice small slivers of flesh from her breasts, her crotch, her belly, like scaling a fish, until her body bubbled like a red carp. Her mouth so thick with pain, she could hardly scream stop it. stop it. stop it.

Today, United States Marines invade Grenada. Why do I think of this woman's life? Like sirens that hurt the ears of dogs, like insidious water dripping through rusty drains, like the pain of flesh slowly slivered and peeled, we want to scream, stop it.

Yesterday, Benigno Aquino, bringing hope home like a day full of poppies, died. Undisguised murder in the open air, his blood darkening into tunnels of the earth. Marcos' assassins pick their teeth, and the day spills the stench of rotten fish. We beat our fists against the windows, weeping in the passageways . . . stop it.

Linette barely lived. The police did nothing. The courts shrugged their shoulders and yawned. When she went home from the hospital, he was waiting, enraged by her acts of defiance. He took his razor and burning cigarette and made her hurt, made her bleed. She knew this time he would show he could control her death. She wanted to survive. The bullet went through his heart, and she thought she saw for the first time in his eyes, surprise that she had made him stop it.

So why do I think of this woman on the day of the invasion in Grenada?

We cannot catch our breath, our tongues too thick with rage, beating our fists against windows. Each day people disappear in Chile, Paraguay, Honduras, Uruguay, Bolivia, Guatemala. Assaults against the sovereignty of Nicaragua. Blockades against Cuba, genocide in El Salvador. Murders in Manila. Apartheid in South Africa.

Each day the ism's like a boot attempt to crush us: racism, capitalism, imperialism, materialism, sexism, colonialism, ageism, classism, militarism.

> We must breathe deeply.
> Escape through the windows.
> We must gather, find each other.
> Hear the heartbeats, the power in our veins.
> We must clear our voices,
> take action to make ourselves known.
> We must stop it
> stop it
> stop it.

RED

For rent.

        I watched
        the chickens circle,

        scratching
        out their code.

        One of the rules
        of the yard
        was to keep
        the red birds
        away from the white flock.

She,
combed neat,
peeked
from shaded windows.

        The Red
        had flown from her coop
        where she was kept
        apart,   now
        surrounded by
        the flock.

She,
sharp eyed
and lidless,
cooed
from the crack
of her door,

There aren't any of you
in this neighborhood.

The flock rushes
and Red
is buried beneath
white feathers flying.
Red's
head bleeding.
Beaks plucking, pecking
crazed by blood.

Old Red.   Dead.

Didn't know her place.

"...IF YOU DON'T WANT TO BELIEVE IT..."

Coffee steaming,
my daughter asleep
safely in the morning.
There are trees outside
that bloom here.
Wind brushes the begonias
dusting mist from
their eyes.
The sun slides
through my blinds
like razors.

Dateline, Johannesburg.
Soldier shoots a nine year old
black child in Soweto.
He thought he was shooting a dog.

A state of emergency.
Toaster burns out,
refrigerator broken,
these gadgets tied to my hands
not to comprehend
wholesale detention, slaughter.
The easy distraction of the blender,
tending of gardens.

A black child
dead.

(Quote from South African Government spokesman, *San Francisco Chronicle*,
June 21, 1986.)

Newsprint flickers
over the sea, the mountains,
the plains of drying bones,
blood flecked corrugated
iron fences.

A black child is dead.
He thought it was a dog.

Dead black child.
Lucifer's smile,
like dead light
with all the care of diamonds
wrapped to our fingers.

Dead black child
mistaken for a dog.
The official response:
". . . if you don't want to believe it,
you don't have to."

His smile glinting like
the cold white stones in his mines.

WHERE IS BEAUTY, IMELDA?

Imelda Marcos says: "Power and strength
is man. Beauty, inspiration, love is
woman. Women have their place in the
home, in the bedroom . . ."

Where is beauty, Imelda?

    Your heart is dead winter
    your words like moldy cake
    undernourishing us.

    You, a rancid rose,
    withered petals between your thighs.

Where is inspiration?

    Your rivers have dried.
    The horses are thirsty.

    The man you prop on a throne is straw,
    swollen from cirrhosis.

    He does not remember
    his own lies.

    Your legs close tightly
    clutching the refuse
    of your country.

Children steal rotting fruit, paper, plastic.
They hunger
like the weather, a beggar that rips
the skin off mangos and defiles
them in the sun.

Your hills are naked, taut
like the people, seedless.

Where is love?

Decadence in the palace.
You dare not open your thighs.
The smell will kill the gardenias
floating in your opulent gardens.

The business of the bedroom, Imelda,
with assassins and aging generals
whose cheeks bloat with fear,
whose fingers shake
and drying flesh chatters
in the wind growing
over darkening mountains.

How will you lock
your bedroom?

How will you conceal

bones of the murdered
sprouting like trees?

How will you stop

    the strength of thunder
    gathering in villages?

How will you explain

    the power
    of rain
    that washes your refuse
    from the shouting streets?

Serafin

You would be proud.

Once you said
yellow was your favorite color
        (next to brown).

We remember your poems
to farmworkers
and manongs
to the murdered and the hungry
of your homeland.

You sang
even with your pain
        (the pain that took you from us)
plucking at you
between your eyes.

Serafin,
the yellow is vast
surging like fields of
buttercups and jonquils
shouting Cory. Cory. Cory.

The Marcoses are gone.
Ferdinand is stuttering
in an empty room.

Imelda speaks and we are
astounded. Amused. She insists all those
shoes belong to the maid.
She sings
to an empty room.

You would be proud.
A woman leads your people.
Cory is strong.
She reminds us of our mothers
who want to fill our stomachs.
She speaks wisely to our enemies.
Her smile is kind.

Look Serafin . . .
All the yellow
clad brown people,
brilliant as the day,
as the hope
that shines from
your poems
about the revolution
that has come.

LOVE CANAL

And you will forget
even this
> the earth
> gray, its sickness
> bubbling
> through the cracked lips
> of packed dirt.
> Maria
> lies in her bed
> lined with mourners,
> suitors, priests, sons.
> In love,
> her eyes dropping
> sorrow,
> her pale gray hands
> thinned to the bone
> fingering the beads,
> hope emaciated like starved
> women.
> Maria,
> mother, lover,
> opening for them
> like a moist cave
> promising tomorrow,
> forever.

And you will forget
even this.
> They wound
> the heart,
> burn, pierce,
> bludgeon the breast
> of Love Canal.
> Her lips, lungs swell,
> heave, spit.

Maria dreams
between her pain,
her skin burning,
cells screaming
armpits glowing
with bright embers
of radiation treatments.
He brought sunshine
like marigolds
into her lap
made her heart pump full
with rhythms of a young colt.
And in the streams
surrounding Love Canal,
they would dip, sip,
deep into each other's skin.
Her body
a canal for love
glistens with pain
sores like water
running to the edges of
her flesh.

And you will forget
even this

       Hooker Chemical Company
       pours the poison
       dumps its waste
       into vessels of earth
       at Love Canal.
       Mothers sip
       from its wells,
       children sleep
       in the fragrant air
       of buried waste,
       fathers infertile
       hum lullabys to unborn.

Maria awakens
from her toxic pillow
wet from the canal
of her polluted body,
flesh aflame,
bubbling pain,
like the angry earth
spewing sickness.

The priests and suitors
pray   fear no evil
            fear no evil
            fear evil
            evil . . .
over her body
once Love's Canal.

REVERSALS

REVERSALS

For Layne

I find myself
now, sending
you words on yellow paper
to share my void,
the fears, the small complaints
that make hairline
wrinkles around my mouth.
I remember
when we searched
as children
in the fields,
in the abandoned
fallen chick houses,
I for insects
to pin to my collection,
my insects, neatly pinned
guarded against you,
in the convent of my room.
Your search
for the streak of gold
in rocks,
black little stones,
joyful, envied by me.
You seemed so fearless
of loss or failure.
A stone cast aside,
worthless, quickly forgotten,
while I,
as if to gather small, irreplaceable
bits of myself,
would stockpile
broken wings,
dismembered limbs
and carefully add
to my collection.

My brother,
I did not know
your manhood would not consume
my barren room,
impaled with dead butterflies.
Nor that your capacity
for joy, your ease
with life
could streak gold
on this small stone,
my heart.

ZIPPER

Stolen breath,
groping in corners,
closets,
barn,
darkened bedrooms while all
is hushed
by sleep
or distance,
his fingers search
the length of her body,
muffled in disgust, fear.
Puberty swelling
in small breasts, squeezed
like spring pears.
Don't.

as the zipper presses
along white mound of bone,
soft flesh.
His tongue flicks to wet
dry lips.
His fingers work the shiny zipper.
No silent prayer,
no whisper of disgrace,
no speechless pain
would keep the teeth
clenched. Zipper
undone.
A jagged sneer across her flesh.

JADE

The woman insisted
my name must be Jade.
Your name's not Jade?
Well, it should be.
It suits you, jewel of the orient.

I knew a young hooker
called Jade.
She had red dyed hair
and yellow teeth
bucked around a perpetual candy bar.
They called her Jade
because she was Clyde's
jewel of the orient.
Her real name was Sumiko . . .
Hardy or Johnson or Smith.
She was from Concord.
Boring, she said,
and kept running away
from home. Her father
would come looking for her,
beat her again,
drag her home
while her mother
babbled and bawled in Japanese.
Concord was boring.
Jade kept running away,
Clyde's jewel of the orient.
He took care of her well,
and she couldn't wait
to see him, her hunger
like locusts in drought,
to put the cold needle to her vein,
blood blossoming in the
dropper like bougainvillea
pushing the heroin through,
her eyes exploding with green lights,

the cold encasing
each corpuscle,
rushing through
heart to the spine,
a freeze settling in each
vertebrae until
she's as cold as stone,
metabolism at zero degrees,
speech center numbed
and life as still as icicles.
Pain, boredom, loneliness
like a frosty pillow
where she lays her nodding
head.

            I wanted to tell
            the woman who kept
            insisting my name was Jade

about Jade.
who od'd. Her jaundiced body
found on her cold floor
mattress,
roaches crawling in her ears,
her dead eyes, glassy
as jewels.

WHO IS SINGING THIS SONG?

                    I am
The Oi River
winding around fields
full with rice waving
bursting with women planting.
I leave with spurts of wind
spilling to the Pacific
great passageway for small boats.

Who is singing this song?

                    I am

The water and air
that dances
on your fingertips,
the water swirling in precise pools
that slake your thirst,
water with tempo, measure,
murmur, licking at your ear.

Who is singing this song?

                    I am

A street veering, connecting
colliding with corners
rolling up/down hills.

Smell me.
rice/adobo
sashimi
imo/juk/gai lon
kimchee.

Hear me.

We survive by hearing.

Who is singing this song?

       I am

We discover each other
our small silences peel open
like roses
We explore the layers of our fears.
       will he   will I   will they   will I not?

We have so long undressed without light
ashamed of our size
the shape of our thighs
the sweep of our eyes.

We survive by hearing
We ignite ourselves from inside

The light surrounds us and we
are surprised.

I seek where and how to touch.

Who is singing this song?

I am

The hands of grandmother, mother
sinewed from work,
blue veined like magnolias
soft as cloth, wiping away
the sweat from men's shoulders
massaging the balms, the lotions
deep into their backs.

I look through family albums
the women's hands clasped like small bouquets,
Umeko, plum blossom child.
Shigemi, luxurious growth of beauty.
Haruko, beautiful spring.
Minoru, treasured son, bearer of fruit.

These hands have yielded me,
palms open, allowing birth,
tying cord, pulling knot
through immigration,
segregation, tribulation,
relocation.

Who is singing this song?

I am

a floating note on a koto
a thunderstorm steady like taiko
I can be heard humming the blues
in rice paddies
and desert camps, unraveling barbed wire
like silkworm thread.

A woman
dancing in the ocean's swell
searching for pearls in the pacific
I string them across my eyes,
my skin the color of moonlight.

I am your own, a child in dark streets,
woman seeking safety in a world of shadows,
I am the present, struggling to be free
a crusader in these spiritless prisons,
pinnacles to greed and sterility.

Who is singing this song?

I am

a survivor
a saboteur of stereotypes
image maker, an endless string of speech.

We survive by hearing.

We discover each other
each of us yielded by hands
of the transplanted,
the escapees, the adventurers
pregnant with dreams.

We explore our similar histories.

We ignite ourselves from inside.

Our hands are warmed, alive.

Who is singing this song?

        I am

pulled by hands of history
to not sit in our times,
complacently, Walkmans plugged to our ears,
computer printouts, soap operas lulling us to sleep.

We are required by these hands of history
to be a storm of hands
that wave in protest
against apartheid, assaults,
invasions, indifference to the poor.
a storm of hands that
dismantle the MX's and the
Tridents and the Pershings and the Cruise missiles.

Who is singing this song?

I am

a river of hands that reach
to the suffering, the suppressed in
South Africa,
the paralyzed in El Salvador,
the starving of Ethiopia, the dying Hibakusha.

a wreath of hands
woven from blossoms shaped from
whispers for justice
over the grave of Vincent Chin.

a sea of beating hands
that persuade patriarchies that
strength is not force
and real power is not oppressing
nor patronizing,
but shared power
among people free, working,
creating, passionate.

Who is singing this song?

I am

We survive by hearing.
We speak to each other.

offering choices

to live, to dream
to extend our hands, to dance
to cringe, to quiver
to kiss, to not kiss.

I dare you
dare you

to love, to dream
to kiss.

We survive by hearing

Who is singing this song?

       I am.

Mama went to Hawaii
for her vacation.
Visited Pearl Harbor.
Brought back bad memories she says,
being Japanese.
Internment camps.

        Diamond Head.
        Polynesian Fantasy.
        Hibiscus Buffet.
        Fire dances.
        Aloha Festival.
        Having a great time.

Pearl Harbor.
Tired me out.

WHEN THERE IS TALK OF WAR

I know I am dying soon. In and out I float like a boat lifted on the shoulders of the sea, pain cresting high like white-capped waves. How many nights I want to let my body slide over the edge into dark, undulating arms, promising nothing.

Teru enters my room with a tray of steaming soup. How strange his smooth-fingered touch. My son, are you not tired of nursing this old woman? Are you not angry with the smell of death, Teru, clinging onto your youthful fingers, permeating this house full with your children?

Remember me once robust and full chested with the juices of health? The day you were born, your father hung blue paper fish, rejoicing that you were a boy. How proud I was I had made him so happy. Your father. Ah, how he would look at me, back then, with love. And the days rippled with joy, like the waves of the fields, as we worked side by side. Sometimes, desire would rise in me so strongly, I would grasp his dirt brown hands and pull him to the watershed where he would hold me. His kisses would linger like cool breezes until the work was done.

Ah, Teru, I remember him too well, and my bed is cold and painful and empty. The tongue of death has licked this wasted body, gutted by memories of dead fish, falling flesh, hair floating in flame, ashes of Hiroshima.

This cruel death wraps me in rasping breath, negating all else . . . nothing else matters . . . only the reality of this pain. Those things which you feel so strongly about, my son, with the idealism of your youth, like peace and justice . . . are nothing.

Where was justice that day when my visit to Hiroshima marked the beginning of my suffering, this solitary journey to my grave? Where

---

"When There Is Talk of War," a fictional prose piece, was inspired by the true story of a Japanese American "Hibakusha"—an atomic bomb survivor who, it is said, went for thirty years without feeling human touch. Because of the unknown nature of radiation sickness then, she feared contaminating her family and friends.

Unlike the survivors of Japan, Japanese American survivors who were trapped in Japan during World War II when the bombs were dropped and who subsequently returned to their homes in the United States, have often been isolated, victimized by the callous neglect of an American government that spent millions on research and construction of nuclear weapons, but nothing on its consequences—including medical research, medical compensation and other support systems.

was justice that day so long ago when innocent ones vaporized, burned, scattered in an instant blaze? Where was justice that hot day in August when death dropped like giant broken wings, sweeping all within its broken flight? A thousand suns soaked into our palms. Memory followed as endless rivers, black with bodies, soaked with weeping. Water turned to vinegar, disbelief, mercilessness.

But I am too tired for bitterness and regret . . . I have only this desire for it to be ended now. I must put those years of hospitals and grim faced medical men behind me, those answerless years of wait and worry.

I want to give you something before I die, my son, that is whole and fresh like the trees outside my window—not this waste of body, this moan I can't suppress, this smell of slow decay. I want to leave you with the memory of me lifting your childbody, carrying you joyfully like a basket of plump radiant peaches from our orchard, blossoms swirling like songs, trees swaying like women in love.

I am wrong, Teru, I have one regret. This throat of death sucking without comfort . . . for thirty years I would not touch you nor your father for fear you would catch this then unknown disease, and I would weep those endless nights with loneliness and fury because I could not cradle my grandchildren, nor laugh with them on my lap, nor kiss their plump faces. Yes, I regret those years empty with not touching, not knowing. Those endless tests. Those endless costs . . . my body ravaged slowly by the cancer of that bombing, they say so now. All those years I could have been comforted by holding your face in my hands, my son. When your father died, I blamed myself. I am so tired, Teru, I wish I could smell the trees outside, or sleep without this pain.

Yes, I am wrong again, my son. Forgive me, but pain makes me so selfish. Peace and justice do matter. If my wasted body speaks nothing else, my son, *remember it when there is talk again of war. Add your single voice to remind them of my grandchildren who have lived with the smell of death. When there is talk again of war, remind them of the blackened mouths of sad dead women; remind them of the hands in flames reaching to a mute heaven; remind them of the cemeteries, the headstones of all our friends, the water filled with dead fish, the poisoned rains. When there is talk again of war, remind them of the absent ones, remind them of our wasted flesh.* Not out of bitterness, my son, but out of compassion. Not for me, my son, but for my grandchildren.

The sleep comes now, like no other. Your father is on this ship that rides my waves. The distance between us lessens. He has waited as he

did in the furrows of our fields, thirsting for my lips and the cool drink
I have made for him. I cannot mend my past and my present, now as
thin as a wing's membrane. Perhaps you can, my son. I will touch the
smile that hides in the corners of your mouth this last time. I will not
cry for those years we spent at distance. I will only hear the peach trees
swaying like women in love. My body is billowing on the great shoulder
of this sea, and I join your father, brilliant as a thousand suns that burn
into this, my darkness.

For Jeannine

Autumn comes
like a buyer of cloth,
her long fingers
touching,
turning orange,
yellow, brown.

taking what she wants,
stretching
the bone taut air.

Her skin crackles beneath
our feet.

        I didn't think anyone wanted me,

bruises pulled
like a sweater around
my neck.

We talk
in the pore tightening air,
branches bare,
about the girl buried in the chill
of prewinter.

We show each other
our mutilated children
in the guise of women
as autumn plucks
at our lips.

Each color,
blue, black, ochre
popping like kisses
on the rib lined flesh,
the puberty soft thighs.

And we muse
how women
keep bruises
hidden
beneath dead
leaves.

JEALOUSY

is a man's prerogative,
a measure of his manhood,
proof of his love for the woman.

jealousy

is forbidden for a woman,
an ungracious emotion
punishable with shame, guilt,
a measure of her insecurity.

When a man is jealous
it is the woman's fault.
She is bitch for causing him self-
doubt or pain, for daring to challenge
his dominion.

When a woman is jealous
it is the woman's fault
for not being attractive/intelligent/charming/
thin enough. Worse, she is manipulative,
controlling, possessive, castrating,
destructive.

Jealous women have been called evil.

Who told us?

our fathers? the psychiatrist?
a lecherous uncle? Mother?

Do they lie?

Do they lie.

TEARING THREADS

Slowly,

light enters
like gauze spilling
on her shoulders.

She sees for the first time
the aging pools beneath his eyes,
the crippled words
from his thinning lips.

It was not she who
caused him to leave.
She who thought herself unlovable,
unworthy.

She remembered
in her bones,
in the fibres of her skin
how she waited
by the telephone
for years, waiting
until she fell asleep
with cords and threads
and distances wrapped
around her throat.

The agony
was the silence,
cruel silence
of unringing telephones,
unanswered mail.

She began to put on layers
of cloth
to keep herself warm.

She read poems about dead fathers
by Sylvia Plath,
stayed close to the oven.

Each year,
another fabric layered
over another
just as her mother
whose lips
were covered by scarves.

She believed
this penance
required of unlovable women.

Today,

sight restored,
she removes her coat.

He is not giant,
hero, king of life
who she created
who could bestow
the gift of happiness,
acceptance.

Simply an aged man
who ran
to the good times,

forgetting the pain
of old cages made from barbed wire
and dust and potato skins
and arranged marriages,

escaping to
the laughter
of good times,

a well-told joke
discreetly whispered,
withheld from the ears
of children.

She unknots her scarves,
the shawls,
the quilted squares
tied together over her arms.

This loosening of garments,
tearing of thread,
uncovering each layer,
revealing her bare skin,
her lips

shedding
shedding

the silence.

WHY IS PREPARING FISH A POLITICAL ACT?

Preparing fish
each Oshogatsu
I buy a gleaming rock cod,
pink, immaculately gutted.
Each year, a respectable fish
that does not satisfy
(hard as I try)
to capture flavors
once tasted.

Grandmother's hands
washing, scaling, cleaning
her fish,
saved each part,
guts, eggs, head.
Her knife, rusted
at the handle screws
ancient as her curled fingers.
Her pot, dented,
darkened, mottled with age
boiled her brew
of shoyu
sweetened with ginger and
herbs she grew
steamed with blood, water.
Nothing wasted.

Someone once tried to sell her
a set of aluminum
pots, smiling too much, called her
mamasan.

Her silence thicker than
steaming shoyu,
whiter than sliced bamboo root
boiled with fish heads.

Preparing fish
is a political act.

SHEDDING SILENCE

Grandfather: Tsuki ga, deta deta . . .
    (Grandfather dances on stage, singing
    traditional folk song)
Bon.
Festival of the Dead.
Fires light the heat of August.
Lanterns guide us home.
Dancers in flowered kimonos
circle, with drum, flute.
Smells of barbeque teriyaki,
sake spilling from barrels.
All the spirits stop
to watch
young girls with brown skin
bare in summer dresses.
Old men stretch their necks
to sing the high notes . . .
    Tsuki ga, deta deta
    Tsuki ga, deta yoi yoi.
Taiko
steady as heartbeats
powerful as thunder.

Chieko: Shina no yoru . . .
    (Chieko enters. She is singing "China Nights."
    She is dressed in white kimono with sea-green
    undergarment. Trailing from her hands is bright
    crimson obi with gold and silver chrysanthemums
    woven in the silk. She is beautiful, pale, hair neatly
    combed into traditional Japanese style, held with
    lacquer combs and wisteria flowers. Grandfather
    catches the end of the obi, holds it taut as Chieko
    wraps it around herself.)

Chieko: Bon Odori
Dance for the Dead.
    Shina no yoru, yo . . .
Obi will tie
around my breasts

wrap tightly my joy,
my sorrow.
Obi will still my fury.
Knot at my heart.
Threads woven
into fine cloth
slashes across my waist,
layer over layer
pulled tight,
tighter,
to conceal my body
thin as a reed,
hollowed, scraped, whittled.
Inside, fermenting flesh,
spoiled fruit the color
of a scraped womb.
Inside, milk souring,
standing water.
I am the song
of the obi,
contained, confined.
Under the binding of silk
are suffocated
wild horses, yellow volcanos,
riverbanks thick with red flowers,
the wind, sleeping in caves.
    Shina no yoru . . .
    I will pour tea,
display my skills
at various ceremony.
My voice and art of dance
will turn the heads
of all men.
One brave warrior
will pause,
sleep in the wide waves
of my kimono sleeves,
and I will comfort him
with my sacrifice . . .
        (She laughs, her voice too shrill)

See, Sansei.
It isn't easy.
> *(Chieko floats off stage, humming "China Nights." Her obi is tightly in place, tied with a wide bow at her waist. Grandfather sits on a short stool, in almost a squatting position. The spot is on his face, made up white, an almost mask like quality.)*

Grandfather: Bon.
Festival of the Dead.
Everyone comes home
gathered for a feast.
The women prepare
norimaki. Teriyaki chicken.
Potato salad.
Corn on the cob.
Sashimi gleaming moist and fresh
in boats of lotus leaves.
Everyone is home
travelling long distances.
Russell, grandson,
Jadine, granddaughter.
Tosh, my drunken son.
Haru, father of my grandchildren.
Michi, my daughter, wife of Haru.
My old wife, lighting incense at the altar,
whispers prayers for me and my poor
daughter, Chieko.
Hiro, grandson, listens to spiders.
> *(Spot comes up on the shape of Hiro, sitting crosslegged near his grandfather, in front of a window. We cannot see his face or size.)*

Hiro: Spiders more fun than anything.
Stretching white threads
across my window.
Waits for flies and moths.
Mommy knits, waiting always
for daddy, who works into the night.
Soon a moth
with red eyes, flies to the window.

Spider quick, bites moth.
Wraps it up for dinner.
Grandmother say never kill spider.
Might kill Grandfather's soul
or Auntie Chieko's.
Spider is ghost of ancestors, spinning
stories in their webs.
(Chieko floats back on stage)

Chieko: Thread
spinning, spinning
into obi,
wrapped tightly,
a reminder to mince steps/words.
Take shallow, quick breaths,
release your sorrow
discreetly, drop by small drop.
(She pulls out a fan and begins her dance,
positioning the fan coyly in front of her face,
flutters it across her body)
He said my beauty was delicate
like ginkgo leaves, small fans
in the wind.
Grace. That's what it's all about.
Grace in failure, in times of need.
Fall gracefully.
Die graciously, quickly
in a cold, white moment.
Because without love,
we are nothing.
Without love
we wither into clumsy uprooted stumps,
cluttering and offensive
to those who need to
get somewhere in a hurry.
(She laughs again, too shrill)
I tell you, Sansei.
It isn't easy.
(Chieko dances to opposite side of stage from
grandfather. She sits on a stool, gracefully, posed.
Her face like a mask, spotted. Lights focus on a

family dining room table, where Jadine and
Russell are alone together.)

Jadine:	So, how's your life, Russ?
Russell:	I'm in love.
Jadine:	Again?
Russell:	She's a dream.
Jadine:	What color?
Russell:	What difference does it make?
Jadine:	Oh. I see.
Russell:	We don't see each other for a year. Still into being *political?*
Jadine:	Does she tell you how much she loves our flower arranging? And those clever little radios we make so well?
Russell:	Not funny, Jay.
Jadine:	Remember the last one you were in love with who expected me to wash her dishes and let Ma wait on her like we were her maids?
Russell:	What the hell's wrong with you?
Jadine:	I ain't white. Don't you know, baby, I got an inferiority complex.
Russell:	Goddam right.
Jadine:	What does she tell you to do, prune her bush, *gardener?*
Russell:	She happens to think I'm a pretty good surgeon. Hey. Sound bitter, sis. Gonna shrivel you up. Unbecoming.
Jadine:	I've never been "becoming" to you, bro.
Russell:	Yeah. I know you. You possessed. A demon of self-hate. You think your looks don't get you over so you gotta compete with me. Kill me, overachiever. Your competence suffocates me. You make me feel . . . small. Who wants that?
Jadine:	You feel equal to a white woman, boy? She got her satin slipper on your neck.
Russell:	If I'm gonna get castrated, better a white woman. They're *supposed* to control us.

(Russell walks out. Angry. Pushes over a chair.
In the backdrop, slides are projected as if on a
t.v. screen. Vogue *covergirl. Voluptuous*

Cosmopolitan *model. Calvin Klein jeans ad.*
Lights dim, single spot on Jadine. She speaks in
flashback, out to the audience.)

Jadine: I had a crush on this white guy, see? He was a track
star. Drove a blue convertible and had gray eyes. He
dated my roommate in college. Becky Blomquist.
God I envied her. One day the track star calls up,
I answer, tell him Becky's not home. And he says
he's calling me. Well, I'm shocked. But I told him
I'd meet him in the back of the library. Wanted all
my buddhahead friends to see me walking off with
him. When he picks me up, the buddhaheads are
snickering. I think, yellow with envy. Me and gray
eyes in his blue convertible. He parks near the
tennis courts, deserted and dark. Starts kissing me.
The night sounds stopped. The air started smelling
of jasmine and silver stars. It was really something.
His hands start up my sweater and he kisses my
breasts. My sweater comes up over my head.
Suddenly all the white lights go on. It was crazy, like
a bomb had dropped and I just didn't hear it. I look
at him and he's smiling like nothing's happening. I
grab for my sweater and bra and I hear the laughter
now like red rain. Three of his friends from the
track team turned on all the big tennis court lights
and he is laughing too. Said they never made it
before with a yellow chick and couldn't I take a joke?
(Spot on Chieko)

Chieko: Bind, knot each thread.
Each stitch in our soul, a scar.
Gook
slopehead
jap
chink
tight eyes
dragon lady
geisha girl.
Don't speak of it.
Pull, wind,
wrap, tie the terror in your throat.

Choke without sound.
Secretly with fingers of genmai,
bonsai breeder,
cherry blossom breath.
Our arms will spin
these silent strings.

(Michi enters dining table set)

Michi:	What's between you and your brother. Fighting again?
Jadine:	No. It's a joke.
Michi:	Why are you so difficult?
Jadine:	You mean why do I say what I think?
Michi:	There are things best not said at all.
Jadine:	You are so protective of your precious son. I will not act as you wish me to.
Michi:	You could be attractive.
Jadine:	Not on your terms.
Michi:	You must learn, women are vulnerable.
Jadine:	You are my beautiful mother. Gracious under insult. Firmly rooted in marriage and family.
Michi:	Don't be sarcastic. Beauty leaves with the years. Mouths are everywhere, sucking at you. Like the lips of air, drying you up.
Jadine:	Beauty and youth should not be everything for a woman.
Michi:	You are not getting younger. We are nothing without a man.
Jadine:	What if I never find a man?
Michi:	Then you are nothing.
Jadine:	Fear sucks at you.
Michi:	Woman is the farm. She lies as a field and all things enter. The rain, the frost, the sun. And we bear. All the slopes and valleys of us are tilled. Peeled open. Excavated. Penetrated.

	And we reproduce.
	This is what we do.
Jadine:	But I am a river.
	Frozen on its surface.
Michi:	The river still flows beneath.
Jadine:	We are afraid for anyone to come
	too close to us,
	afraid they will crack us open
	and we will drown them.
Michi:	You do not resemble me at all.
Jadine:	I am not your monument, your legacy.
	Do you not long for something that
	is your own?
	That has been made by your hands,
	the light from your passion,
	the fire from your imagination?
	Something of you?
Michi:	No, you are not my monument.
	My son is.
	(Dark)
	(Spot on Grandfather,
	Chieko)
Grandfather:	Man and woman
	like rock and water.
	Water must flow around rock.
	Eventually, wears it to sand.
Chieko:	Women, dangled
	from thread,
	rope.
	Wrapped in smothering cloth
	to hide our openings,
	our shoreless heart.
	We are locks without keys,
	a convent wall,
	a saltless sea.
	(Dark)
	(Lights up on Russell and Tosh)
Russell:	That stuff will kill you.
Tosh:	*(Waving his bottle)* Smart boy. Teach you that in
	medical school?

Russell:	Well, it's *your* liver.
Tosh:	My liver loves it. My ahtama *(pointing to his head)* loves it. And it loves me. Better than a woman.
Russell:	Your batteries dead, unc?
Tosh:	Hey. It's festival time, boy. She gives me a good time. *(waves bottle)* She lets me sleep. Lets me say what I want to say. Doesn't ask for more than I'm willing to give. Doesn't nag me with guilt or weakness. She don't terrify me with purity, or threaten to withhold her body. She don't require performance or perfection. She lets me sleep.
Russell:	We climb out of their bellies worn, little old men. Even when we beat them, they try to make us feel strong. Coax us up again. Try to make us feel safe so we'll climb back in.
Tosh:	Life's dangerous, boy. Women can mix you up. They scream about wanting independence, but complain when you leave them alone. They say they want respect, but get mad when you don't come on strong. They call us self-centered when we tell them what to do but despise us for being weak when we ask them what they want.
Russell:	Pass the bottle, unc.
	(Dark on Russell and Tosh. Lights up on women who are preparing sushi. Michi ladles steaming rice into a large bowl, pours sweet vinegar, stirring it into the rice. Jadine is cooling the vinegared rice with a fan. Grandmother is filling the brass altar cups with rice to place on her altar. Spot on Grandfather and Chieko.)
Grandmother:	Obon. Festival of the dead. The fires burn to guide us home. Ghosts are hungry journeying far. Sitting at the feast, they stir the brew of memory.
Jadine:	Your sons. Ma. How is Hiro your legacy?

Michi: I keep losing everything.
                Have you seen the ladle with
                dented handle?
                My lacquer bowl?
                My pale green china vāse.
                Everything just disappears.
Jadine: What happened to Hiro?
Michi: My red silk scarf.
                The flowers I cut this morning.
                Have you seen them?
Jadine: Ma. Why don't you ever talk about
                the camps?
Michi: Lost. The sugar cannister.
                The cast iron pan.
                Where are the teacups with blue leaves?
                See the orchard? Apples used to be
                bigger than his fists.
                All shriveled and sour.
Grandmother: We carried so many dreams with us.
                Over the ocean. The canefields.
                You cannot imagine the work.
                Before dawn would light our way,
                we were awake, boiling water,
                cooking.
                And then out into the sugar cane
                that ripped open our hands
                and broke his back.
Michi: More work when we arrived here.
                But we were just getting somewhere.
                Then Mrs. H's husband disappeared.
                She thought he was dead in a ditch.
                Hit by a car. Shot by a thief.
                Huh. He was detained by the military.
                She didn't see him until after the war.
Grandmother: We could have been bitter.
                Our mouths wrinkled and spitting up
                sighs of defeat.
Jadine: I want to know about the camps.
Michi: The camps?

Just before the war, you were born. I thought it might be better to go see one of those women who do their business in the dark, plucking babies out of wombs with tweezers and coat hangers and hot wire sterilized by candlefire.
We were so poor. Anything not to bring another mouth into the world.
Fan the sushi rice.

Jadine: I'm fanning.
Michi: But I had you anyway. Fan!
Jadine: I'm fanning.
Grandmother: You were a beautiful baby girl.
Michi: What calamity. I thought my mother-in-law would die.
Keep fanning, (voice angry).
Jadine: I'm fanning.
Michi: A girl. Your father was so disappointed. Thank god Hiro and Russell came along. What would he have done if I didn't give him sons.
Grandmother: You were a happy baby.
Michi: Why, I'll never know. Well, what do you know but they bombed Pearl Harbor.
Jadine: And we were sent to camp.
Michi: We knew we were really in trouble.
Keep fanning.
Faster! (voice angrier)
Jadine: I'm fanning, I'm fanning.
Michi: My mother-in-law hated me. Said I was stuck up. I think she was jealous because I didn't look so Japanese. I tried to make her accept me. One day she shaved your head.
Grandmother: You had such beautiful thick curly hair.
Michi: Not like most nihonjin babies with straight ugly pricks of hair. She was jealous. Well that just got to me and I ran to my barrack and cried all day.
Keep fanning. Faster.
Jadine: (softly) The camps?
Grandmother: (Takes the sushi rice to the altar)
Namu amida butsu. Namu amida butsu.

	(Dark except on Grandfather and Michi who *walks into a single spot. She seems lost in memory,* *speaking to no one directly)*
Grandfather:	It happened this way.
Michi:	We had gotten adjusted the best we could in those hot barracks. I was miserable. Big and pregnant again. My father was agitated because of our terrible diet. He'd roam around in the dust, kicking it in the air. I was so worried about him.
Grandfather:	Mushitte wa Mushitte wa gathering, gathering dust like memory swirling it in the wind.
Michi:	Papa was really angry this time. I felt responsible. He asked the camp authorities to give me some food with protein.
Grandfather:	Silence is a form of strength. More is said with wordless defiance.
Michi:	Papa was furious. They refused him. He's so proud. Hated to ask in the first place. He picked up a handful of sand and threw it toward the fence. The guard picks up his rifle.
Grandfather:	If we bend to foreign ways we do so as a matter of practicality. This is how we survive.
Michi:	I try to calm Papa. He's working himself into a rage. I'm really afraid. Days of nothing but rice and rutabaga. Rumor was the camp authorities had secreted a load of fowl. It seemed they deliberately wanted to starve us. The tower guard is smiling, aiming his rifle. I'm screaming at Papa. PAPA! He's running toward the guard, fists full of sand. I am sure I will hear the deafening crack. I can feel the bullet tear through my back. I can see Papa's body shattered, bloodied. My mouth opens. No sound comes out.
Grandfather:	We are here to be tested. We earn humanity with each burden we endure.

Michi:	Papa turns and throws the fistful of sand toward the tower and raises his shaking fist. I am sure I will see the bullet go through his heart and mine as I rush toward his side. I look for wounds. He is shaking in rage. I look up at the tower guard. He is laughing.
Grandfather:	Pine in winter.
	Bamboo in storm.
	We do not wither or break.
	(Dim spot on Hiro at his window. We still cannot clearly see his size.)
Hiro:	The spider is spinning very fast.
	Web is repaired.
	prepared for next victim.
	I will capture flies.
	(Dark on Hiro. Chieko walks into spot, unwrapping her obi, folding it carefully. Her kimono is loose, revealing contemporary dress.)
Chieko:	Threads of ourselves,
	tied to history. Our journeys.
	Body of my father, an abandoned farm.
	Face of my mother, paper thin.
	White voices like the tip of bayonets.
	Barbed wire wraps us in time,
	wraps us as a shroud.
	(Chieko remains in spot.
	Lights up on the three women
	near the dining table.)
Grandmother:	Namu amida butsu.
	Play music. Chieko's songs.
Jadine:	Auntie Chieko who died so young?
Michi:	She ruined herself. Madness. Cigarettes. Starvation.
Jadine:	Not normal.
Grandmother:	She had a dream.
Michi:	She wasted all your money for a stupid dream. None of us can make it in their world.
Jadine:	The camps.
Grandmother:	She wanted to be a star.
Jadine:	Racism.
Michi:	Will you shut up, Jadine! Chieko was foolish. She wasted herself.

Grandmother:	Grandfather loved her. He wanted only to hear her sing.
Michi:	And neglected the rest of us. We who worked so hard for you to send *her* to New York.
Grandmother:	She was beautiful. So talented.
Michi:	So mad.
Grandmother:	Please wind up the phonograph.
	For Bon.

(Jadine winds the old-fashioned phonograph, Grandmother's treasured antique. As the music plays, the lights dim on the three women. The music is Puccini's "Madame Butterfly," Cio Cio's aria "One Fine Day." Spot is solely on Chieko. She pulls a bag close to her, packs the obi, pulls clothing out, drops them on the floor, packs them again. Speaks directly to audience.)

Chieko: I am Cio Cio san.

Miss Nakano to you.

Excuse me, but I must begin my make up now. Hold all my calls, except for Joe, of course.

(Chieko starts to put on her make up, painting eyeliner, lipstick as she practices her scales.)

La la la la la la

Ahhhh ahhhhh (melody line from aria)

No. They can't turn me down this time.

(Chieko holds various pieces of clothing from her bag up to her body, discards them, puts them back in her bag.)

Joe served in the Army. Was sent to occupied Japan. He says the most beautiful women in the world are from the Orient. He was tempted to bring one home. But was glad he didn't because he met me. Right here in New York.

If father knew, he'd have a fit, me dating a hakujin. Ahhhh ahhhhh *(continues melody line)*. Oh, you Sansei. You have it easy now. You can marry anyone you want. They even have movies and plays with all oriental casts. Imagine that! When I started out, I was the only one trying to make it in the opera world. They tried to discourage me.

Huh. Miss Nakano to you.

But I don't give up easily.

They wouldn't let me stay in certain places . . . so
many people still hated the *Japs* they'd call me.

Miss Nakano to you.

Have I received any phone calls?

Joe says we really know how to take care of our men.

When we met, he asked me out to dinner. *(whispers)*
I was starving, being on such a strict budget.

We went to this little Italian restaurant where they
played opera music. It was so romantic.

> *(Chieko sings another line from Butterfly's love
> song. She dances in her spotlight with her hands
> clasped.)*

Well, confidentially, we went to a hotel. I was so
embarrassed. He told the clerk I was his warbride.

Joe believed in me. Encouraged me. Said I'd be the
first Nisei opera star in America.

> *(Chieko sings a little more fiercely. Her voice begins
> to crack slightly.)*

At my audition they kept mispronouncing my name.
Nakamuu, Nakaow, Nakenoo. Huh.

I just sang my heart out anyway.

Joe made me feel beautiful, like a star.

I loved to please him.

I'd massage his back for hours.

> *(Chieko pulls the obi from her bag, caresses it as
> she slowly unfolds it.)*

You liberated Sansei women might laugh but let me
tell you, a man wants to be treated like a king.

> *(Chieko sings again, her voice sounding slightly
> more strained.)*

Yes, we've paved some roads for you, and our feet
have bled. I'll tell you, it hasn't been easy.

> *(Chieko's voice changes to a nasal, flat, voice unlike
> her own.)*

[Stage manager:] Miss. O Miss. You're not scheduled
to audition. The cast has been selected. Don't recall
any, uh, orientals in this production. Please. Off the
stage.

(Chieko responds to the voice she has created, turns to stage right.)

Miss Nakano to you.

(Chieko sings another line from Butterfly's song, her voice showing much more intensity.)

I'm expecting a very important phone call.

Joe and I would have to be careful where we went together. There was so much prejudice . . .

(Chieko's voice changes again to hostile, flat twang.)

[Stage manager:] Hey. Lady. You'll have to clear the stage.

(Chieko shakes the obi she is holding toward the created voice, stage right.)

N A K A N O! You won't forget it when it's in lights. Father will be proud. He's sacrificed so much for me. And you. Sansei. It's not easy.

Where's my purse? *(searching, snatching it up frantically)* They're always trying to steal something from you.

(Chieko pulls out a handkerchief from her purse.)

Joe gave me this handkerchief. With lace on the borders. Had to use it to stop the bleeding after my uh, umm operation.

(Chieko's voice changes to one of rage, impatience, shouting)

[Stage manager:] Hey you! Get off the stage!!!

(Chieko is now grotesque. Her kimono disheveled, her make up running, clownish, a parody of exaggerated "orientalized" features with black eyeliner curving her eyes to her temples. She sings a line from the suicide aria, and her voice chokes on the high notes. She throws the obi across the stage.)

MISS NAKANO TO YOU!!!

(more softly) Are you ready for my solo?

I don't have all day. I'm expecting a very important phone call.

(Chieko's head is high. She is posed as a true opera star, almost haughty in her pride.)

See, Sansei? It isn't easy.

(Lights up on Grandfather. As he speaks, Chieko walks to him, hands him the end of her unfurled obi. She as if in a ritual, dresses in her kimono, wrapping the obi neatly, as he holds it taut.)

Grandfather: Bon.
Fires flicker, lighting the way
for the dead, returning home.
The dead circle, seeking
solace.
Embers of dreams unfulfilled,
one by one,
each gathering,
each expire in me.

(Lights up on Michi and Jadine at dining table.)

Jadine: I never want to get married.

Michi: With your mouth, you won't have to worry about it.

Jadine: Relationships, Ma. That means relating . . . to each other.

Michi: A man is security. Without a husband, you shrivel up like a sour plum. No grandchildren. An infertile desert.

Jadine: Times are changing. Marriage is outdated.

Michi: Everyone must have a family. When the world spits on you, you can turn to your family.

Jadine: *(aside)* Even they will reject you.

Michi: Only your family really cares.

Jadine: *(aside)* Except for the ones in the litter who are unacceptable, who hold up mirrors of someone you don't want to see.

Michi: There is nothing like the joy of your children . . . watching them grow, fulfilling their needs . . .

Jadine: *(aside)* Some are sacrificed . . . for the favor of others. Aren't females always sacrificed for the well-being of the tribe?

Michi: Good children will take care of you in your old age.

Jadine: Children grow up and leave . . . the ones who survive.

Michi:	Not if they've been raised properly. My children are mine forever.
Jadine:	It is no wonder we are lonely.
Michi:	Do you know about loneliness?
	The feel of empty rooms, swallowing you? No warmth. No sound. No comfort? You do not know if you exist. So you talk to the mirrors. The wall. The sink.
Jadine:	Being ignored or locked up.
	Being expendable.
Michi:	We'll do anything to escape loneliness.
Jadine:	Search for mothers and fathers and brothers who will accept you?
Michi:	A family . . .
Jadine:	What about love?
Michi:	Love matters less as you grow old.
Jadine:	I'm getting very depressed.
Michi:	You find someone who it seems will fill your life like that piece of sky that fits perfectly over the trees in your field. Sleeves for your bare branches. A garment in winter. We'll do anything to get that. So when the years shrivel and children grow and war and distances and work wears the sleeves of love, lonely is patches on sheets washed thin, a sleepless night sky. Lonely is when he doesn't feel when he touches or talk when he speaks, when words are too familiar like "rice," "tea" or "too tired." But you remember the terror of talking to the sink, so you put up with the less empty pain of complaints about cold food and sick chickens and backaches. Your comfort is knowing your bed is not empty.
Jadine:	I want more than that.
Michi:	First get a man.
Jadine:	Ma! I don't want what you got.
Michi:	WHAT WILL PEOPLE THINK???
Jadine:	That I'm not respectable.
Michi:	I'm your mother. I want you to have security. Why did we spend all that money on your education?
Jadine:	So I could find a good husband?

Michi:	You're getting too old to catch a man.
Jadine:	*Catch* a man . . .
	(Lights up on Russell, Haru, Tosh. They are standing stage opposite from the women, facing each other.)
Russell:	Independent women.
Haru:	Smart mouth. See what it gets her.
Tosh:	All the answers and an empty bed.
Michi:	Die an old maid.
Jadine:	Hey, ma. I've tried.
	The lawyer who graduated from Yale.
Michi:	He was from a good family.
Jadine:	He kept combing his hair.
Russell:	Listen to his every word. Pretend he's brilliant.
Haru:	Wear white.
Tosh:	Don't let him in your pants until after two dinners.
Michi:	He would want a good wife.
Jadine:	No, dessert.
Michi:	Lots of nice men out there.
Jadine:	The intern who talked about his sports car.
Russell:	Choose your words. Seem vulnerable. Smile a lot. Cling.
Haru:	Keep the knees locked together.
Tosh:	Don't open them until the war is over.
Jadine:	The engineer from U.C.
Michi:	Invite him to dinner.
Jadine:	I hate silent movies.
Russell:	Make him think he's the center of the world. Be obedient, trustworthy, faithful.
Haru:	Wear the dress with buttons that lock.
Tosh:	No one wants damaged goods.
	(Lights dark on the men. Stage dims, spot on Jadine.)
Jadine:	The sound of shakuhachi
	is oozing around my mind.
	(Traditional shakuhachi or flute music plays softy in background.)
	Beautiful samurai warrior
	squared in the snow,
	with eye-blinking speed

sliced the wind
and his opponent,
blood bursting the cold air.
His woman is looking on
in the high field,
breasts heaving,
obi flying.
He squares his back,
sheathes his sword, locks his hands,
shoulders keeping time
to his leaving her behind.
Toshiro.
You don't ever get down
with your women.
Why don't you?
I can really get into you
sitting in that meditation room alone,
sifting the thoughts of your ancestors,
mind and body
one with your sword.
But.
Must you scorn her all the time?
Don't misunderstand . . .
I really dig
that ritual,
that clear, clean blade
of discipline,
that taut wire
connected to the Way of the Warrior.
Your gathering all time
into moment beyond all time,
that put/feeling/aside
oneness with nature/self
perfectly in tune
    like the
        "bell ringing in an
        empty sky"
    like the
        flute crying alone
    like the

sound of sun on
stone.
And oh, Mifune.
You are so fine
I can sit with you for hours
and wait
and wait
for that climax,
for that instant whipping of your blade
chhhhhaaaaaap!!!
but as you walk off
in the wind blown lonely
twilight,
without even looking back,
your high, wide
stepping in time
to Japanese cowboy music,

I am that woman
kimono clad,
silent and motionless
(except for heaving breast)
suppressing all the frustration/emptiness
not wanting that loneliness

I am that hair
tearing, hara-kiri prone,
longing/licking
body-burning-for-you
woman of the dunes.

Turn around, Mifune!!
Stop cleaning your blade.
We can make
an eternity
together.

(*Dark on Jadine. Lights
gradually up on Michi.
Jadine enters light.*)

Michi: You better think about the future, starting your own family before it's too late.

Jadine: I've got my work.

Michi: You call that work? All that political stuff. Where's it going to get you? Who cares about what happened over thirty-five years ago? Ancient history. And what you call it? Civil rights cases? We've come a long ways. Don't make trouble for yourself.

Jadine: There's trouble, Ma, anyway. We haven't come that far. Don't fool yourself. Who's still at the bottom of the American heap? We just climb over each other . . .

Michi: Enough! No one cares if you're poor and old. You'll never catch a man with your mouth . . .

Jadine: My mouth!
It betrays me.
It has its own life.
I paint it, set it in a smile.
Clamp both hands over it.
Pinch the lips together.
My tongue climbs out between
my fingers.
Pounces on the poor man.
He sees how grotesque it is.
It takes him by surprise.
I try to retrieve it, put it in its place.
It escapes again.

Michi: Don't be sarcastic with me.

Jadine: Never, Ma. It's like having warts. You don't choose to have them . . . thoughts just popping out.

Michi: I've struggled by myself too, Jadine. It was frightening. I thought I would die and no one would know . . .

Jadine: There are different kinds of death. I have to choose my own.

Michi: You're on dangerous ground.

Jadine: Life's dangerous, Ma.

	(Lights dim. Spot on Chieko. She dances with obi in her hands while she tells a parable.)
Chieko:	The youngest daughter of a poor farmer was sold to a wealthy old man. The old man was afraid the girl would run away so he tied her waist with a rope, the other end tied to his wrist. Even when he slept, he kept the rope taut between them. He treated her kindly, but would not release the rope, tugging it constantly to reassure himself that she was present. When the old man died, his son inherited his house and the servant girl. The son prided himself in being more modern and liberal than his father, kept the rope tied to the young servant girl's waist, but lengthened it so that she would have more freedom of movement. She was even able to wander far into the fields and riverbanks by herself. But the young servant girl, without the constant tautness between her and her master, mourned deeply. The son, who could not understand her sorrow, loosened the rope more and more. Finally, the girl threw herself in the river and drowned, miles of loose rope floating above her.
	(Lights up on Tosh and Russell. As they speak. Chieko in dim light floats to Grandfather, hands him the end of the obi and repeats the ritual of wrapping.)
Tosh:	Between the nunnery and nymphomania . . .
Russell:	We try to keep them trembling . . .
Tosh:	To hide, conceal that we are afraid.
Russell:	We can't let it go, the wire we hold taut . . .
Tosh:	On which they walk, balanced . . .
Russell:	Or ever reveal our fear . . .
Tosh:	Never. *(Walks downstage to spot)* I wake up in the middle of the night. Sweating. My mouth is wide open. But there is no noise. No breath. It's like I am drowning.
Russell:	Drowning . . . *(joining Tosh downstage)*
Tosh:	The scream is underwater. Only silent bubbles stream from my mouth. My lungs are bursting.
Russell:	But don't let on.

Don't feel.

Sometimes when I was a little boy, I'd call out for my father in the night. Scared, imagining shadows moving in the dark.

And SHE would come.

Whisper to me not to wake him up. If he hears, he'll tell me to act like a man.

Tosh: Water filling my lungs my hands clutching at anything to pull myself up. Nothing but water. Water.

Russell: Eyes like steel.

He couldn't stand to see me cry.

Even when I was five years old. Damn.

Called me ona . . . woman . . .

Tosh: They called me Jap.

Russell: Ona. Only woman is afraid.

Tosh: *(whispering)* Jap.

There's one of you!! *(Jumping up to foot of stage)* Goddamn yellow sonofabitch. Sneaky motherfucker. Nah. Not one of my relatives. I'm an American.

Russell: And I couldn't fight back.

Tosh: Couldn't fight back.

Russell: *(now also at foot of stage, hand to forehead, saluting audience)* "You are not being accused of any crime . . ."

Tosh: They first put me in mess. I cooked for them. They wanted me to taste the food first. Afraid I'd poison them.

I was their "translator" when they'd break radio code. But they made me cook for them.

Russell: "You should be glad to make the sacrifice to prove your loyalty . . ."

Tosh: When I refused to taste the food, they jammed it in my mouth, pushed my head back like a chicken's.

Russell: "It's your contribution to the war effort . . ."

Tosh: And they'd laugh. While I choked and they shoved more food in my mouth. I flopped like a fish, vomiting.

Russell: "There may be one of you who threatens our national security . . ."

Tosh:	I told them to kill me outright.
	Throw me in the ocean
	so I could float back home to ports of
	California. Beach myself like a whale. Let
	the gulls eat my heart.
Russell:	*(pointing to the audience)* One among you is
	dangerous.
Tosh:	But they just laughed.
Russell:	*(still pointing)* You are dangerous.
	(Dark on Russell and Tosh. Spot on
	Grandfather and Chieko. Lights dimly on
	Haru and Michi at dining table.)
Grandfather:	Bonsai, twisted
	bent, shaped by the wind.
	These trees
	made stronger by adversity.
Chieko:	Why does the slavegirl
	not cut the rope? Untie herself?
	Why does it take you
	so long to ask?
	Cut the rope!
Haru:	Hey, Michi. The baby's crying.
Michi:	No, I just looked in on him. He's fine. Playing
	quietly.
Haru:	He's a good son. Going to be somebody.
Michi:	Maybe he should stay here on the farm with us.
	You're not getting any younger, Haru.
Haru:	No, he's not going to be a farmer. Get his hands
	dirty. Too hard this work. Better for him to go to
	college.
Michi:	And he'll buy all the things we can't afford now. A
	new kitchen. Hiro will get me a stainless steel sink
	with a garbage disposal.
Haru:	We'll go fishing together in a boat with a motor.
	China Lake. A strong boat. So I won't worry about
	drifting out too far.
Michi:	And silk dresses. Like Clara's that float in the breeze.
	(Tosh enters. They stop talking instantly.)
Tosh:	You fantasizing about Hiro again? How he's gonna
	win the Nobel Peace Prize?

Haru:	When are you leaving? You've outstayed your welcome.
Tosh:	That's the trouble when you're trying to hide. We keep finding you.
Haru:	Good for nothing. A drunk! I don't know how we've put up with you this long.
Michi:	Please. You'll disturb Hiro.
Tosh:	Disturb Hiro? I'm not in your fantasyland. You can't disturb Hiro.
Haru:	Shut up! Drunkard.
Tosh:	Bon. Festival of the dead. You buried the past.
Haru:	Get out.
Tosh:	Kind sister. I will leave. But your suffering. End your suffering. Take Hiro to get help.
Michi:	*(Is crying)*
Haru:	*(Furious)* Don't talk like that in this house. Your damn mouth. What it get you? Your wife left you. Ha. Probably for another man. Don't blame her.

> *(Michi moves to step between Tosh and Haru. Tosh is angry, stumbling, swaying, swinging his fists at Haru. Haru grabs his shirt. Russell, Jadine, Grandmother rush in. Pulling them apart. Music from offstage plays softly. A traditional Japanese lullaby. All freeze.)*

Grandmother:	Namu amida butsu.

> *(Everyone is still and watches as Hiro. a grown man, chases his rubber ball. He jumps, claps in child-like movement as he catches it, drops it, laughing as a child. He drops the ball and chases it off stage. Lights dim.)*

Grandmother:	Namu amida butsu.
Chieko:	Rope, wire, threads of silk,
	umbilical cords
	tied to our hearts.
	The past is bound
	gagged, stifled, smothered.
	Air cut off.
	Corridors cobwebbed
	lead to endless deserts.
	Swamps that lie

like a trap.
Spider's silk like barbed wire
awaiting lunch.
Cut the rope.

> *(Slide on backdrop of rows of barracks. Stage is*
> *dark except for Michi lying on a cot spotted in a*
> *barren room. She is obviously in pain of labor.*
> *Grandmother and Haru are present with her.)*

Grandmother: They won't come?

Haru: The nurse at the infirmary said, "babies are born
every minute."

Grandmother: Heartless as these barren deserts.

Haru: They're busy. We have to wait they said.

Grandmother: This is not good. Birth delayed too long.
The baby will not turn without help.
Michi is losing strength.

Haru: *(pacing)* We'll name him Hiromi.
"Beautiful abundance."

Grandmother: I'm afraid for this child.

Haru: We'll call him Hiro. Strong boy.

> *(Slide fades, stage dark.*
> *Lights up on present family.)*

Grandmother: Namu amida butsu.

Tosh: Yea, the casualties were very high.

Haru: Please. Get out.

Grandmother: We brought so much with us.
Dreams. Children.
Dreams for Grandchildren.
Gave up everything.
Picked up. Moved on.
Built again.

> *(Slides of train carload of people. It is the past.*
> *Relocation trains. Jadine and Russell walk into the*
> *slide, juxtaposing past and present.)*

Jadine: It's funny. When everyone is suffering . . .

Russell: We help each other . . .

Grandmother: We were all in shock. Five days to sell everything. Pack
what we could carry. No one knew what to expect.
Your mother was pregnant. Sick. Strangers were
compassionate. Shared their water. An old woman

	rubbed your mother's aching back. We did not know who she was and your mother wept at her kindness.
Russell:	I guess we see ourselves in these times. At first, I was really mad that we didn't fight back.
Jadine:	Really mad.
Russell:	What would we have done?
Jadine:	Same thing, back then.
Russell:	So who are you mad at now, Jadine? The world?
Jadine:	Born in America. Can't ignore the wounds.

(Slide fades. Lights up on present family.)

	Not even you, bro.
Russell:	Your crusading's like a corset.
	Shit. You're cold.
Jadine:	My anger is comfortable to me. Makes me think I'll survive.
Russell:	Survive what? You got out alive. What've you got to fight?
Jadine:	Not you, I hope.
Russell:	You think you're oppressed.
	By everybody.
Jadine:	No. I know *their* indifference like the feel of shiver on my skin. Their eyes are glassy, opaque. Blind to me. I vanish before them like water in the desert. But to you, I am unacceptable.
Russell:	Power structures don't give a shit about your search for significance.
	Me . . . you make me feel uncomfortable.
Jadine:	Russ, I don't want to push you away. I don't want to be a victim to society either. My anger's become comfortable. It's how I measure myself.
Russell:	Society measures us in terms of power. Power is my Porsche, my credit rating, the girl on my arm. My house, my paintings, my ability to buy visibility.
Jadine:	A comfortable existence.
Russell:	It's my choice. You make me squirm when you're my mirror, sis.
	Because then, I feel as invisible as you.
Jadine:	Who did the job on us? Those who orchestrate suffering.
Russell:	Those who we have to prove ourselves to.

Jadine:	No, that's you, bro.
Russell:	Then who do we have? Where do we go?
Jadine:	To the ones who share the suffering.
Tosh:	Hey! You two. It's party time.
Jadine:	Gotta open up the wounds. Let them breathe. This family's festering.
Russell:	Give it a rest, Jay.
Tosh:	Personally, I think open wounds should be treated with alcohol, right Doc?
Russell:	Not total submersion, unc. You'll drown.
Tosh:	Funny guy.

(Spot on Grandfather and Chieko.)

Grandfather:	Memory is the stick that is used to beat you. Keep you alert. Watch your back.
Chieko:	Miles of cord floating above you. Cut the rope.
Jadine:	Secrets.
Russell:	Say something.
Tosh:	Terrible.
Russell:	The void.
Jadine:	I want to know. It's my story, too.
Russell:	Dark rooms. Shadows moving.
Jadine:	Not normal. My mother's shame. Deep, scathing . . .
Michi:	His life, hidden in dark corners whispered in cobwebs . . .
Grandmother:	Truth, boiling like light, no doctors, no boiling water . . .
Haru:	In camp we were not trusted with cooking fire . . .
Grandmother:	The child came out, pushing with terrible rage against being enclosed, encaged . . .
Michi:	Pushed back in . . .
Grandmother:	Mada, Mada sono toi denai

Michi:	It isn't time.
	It isn't time.
Haru:	He broke the chain, the cord,
	smothered in his mother's cage,
	smothered his brain . . .
Grandmother:	He, we
	came out again . . .
Jadine:	Not normal.
Tosh:	The taint
	not in his brain.
Grandmother:	To uso
	To haji
	fukaku chi no naka ni . . .
Russell:	The lies,
	the shame,
	blood deep.
Tosh:	Japanese in prison camps . . .
Jadine:	Not normal at all.
Tosh:	Came back from the army, a war hero.
	Showed my loyalty. Proved I was a man.
	They couldn't break me.
	I thought about my wife a lot.
	Helped get me through the rough times.
	She was pregnant.
	Insisted it was mine.
	(Tosh counts on his fingers to twelve)
	I couldn't sleep after that.
Jadine:	We can't count the losses.
Russell:	Can't bring back the losses.
Michi:	Remember what's important now.
Haru:	What's important . . .
Hiro:	*(Enters weeping)* Spider's gone.
Russell:	Gone to lay her eggs.
Michi:	She'll be back.
Hiro:	I wait by the window
	where she spins across the sky,
	she ties thread to my waist
	and tells me to hide.
	The wind whirls me up
	over fields where lilies grow,

	over the riverbanks
	where water curls like rope.
	Wait by the window
	and she'll spin across the sky,
	Dew rests on her threads
	like tears in my eye . . .
Chieko:	Silk thread spun.
	Wrapped in obi,
	rope, cord.
	These bodies
	a tight winter cocoon.
	Spring comes like a hand
	untying knots,
	slowly, we unwrap, emerge.
	Reveal ourselves.
Grandmother:	We didn't complain.
	Injustices were great.
	Didn't throw up our hands
	and relent to despair,
	choke on strings of sorrow.
	We did not make ourselves extinct.
	We stayed. Rightfully our place.
	Namu amida butsu.
Michi:	Thirty-eight years of not talking about it. Keeping quiet. I can't forget it. Don't want to. What they did to my son. Can't change it, but don't want them to forget it either.
Haru:	The smell was terrible in those stalls. We did the best we could. Dug around and pulled up manure. Treated worse than animals. Your mother kept us together. She had guts. Wrote to authorities. Had guts.
Jadine:	Reparations. No more camps.
Russell:	Dangerous shit, man. Sitting on the sidelines. Keeping quiet. Can't be quiet no more.
Tosh:	Shit no.
Hiro:	Spiders are weaving stories.

> *(Chieko floats into spot. She is beautiful once more. Neatly combed as before, completely dressed in white kimono and tied obi.)*

Chieko:	One end of obi held in his hands. The other end, I will wrap into thin red stem, my face the blossom. I tell you the story, loosening knots, unraveling tangles. Various ends of string floating in the wind. I unravel, cut, bind, unwrap. Forever finding another loose end. But I can sing. As I constantly pull, constantly mend, I sing. I tell you, Sansei. It isn't easy.
Grandfather:	Webs of memory. Songs. Stories that scream from our hearts split in two. Bon. Festival of the dead. I travel in the smoking embers, Chieko's songs shaped from desert flowers, shell, stone. Sand gardens swirling into eternity.
Russell:	We are strange. Haru would make me wake up at five in the morning to go gardening with him. Because he wanted me to become a surgeon. Suffer from the bottom and look up. Never forget the bottom. The suffering. Japanese are funny that way.
Jadine:	Ma would re-wrap my Christmas presents and give them to someone else. She said she couldn't stand the humiliation of getting and not giving. Japanese are funny that way.

Tosh:　There are things we want to forget but we can't. So
　　　we pretend for a long time they didn't happen.
　　　Japanese are funny. *(laughs)*
　　　Don't want to make anybody
　　　uncomfortable.

Grandmother:　Plant the seeds.
　　　Grow the crops.
　　　Harvest its yield, Sansei.
　　　Justice will be done.

Michi:　Hiro is sleeping.
　　　　　　　　(sings traditional Japanese lullaby)
　　　　　Nennen kororiyo
　　　　　Okoro riyo.
　　　Sleep little child
　　　though there's trouble at the gate.
　　　Your father's in potato fields
　　　and won't be home till late.
　　　When the gate is opened, we will again be free.
　　　This land is yours and mine as far as we can see.

Haru:　At the window, he plays,
　　　cobwebs he won't let me sweep away,
　　　watching spiders spinning all day.

Tosh:　Hiro is timeless, like the moon.

Grandmother:　Namu amida butsu.

Jadine:　Bon. Festival of the dead.
　　　Come home.
　　　Unbury the past. Lay it to rest.
　　　Work to be done tomorrow.

Russell:　Give it a rest, Jay. Your mouth.

Jadine:　Watch out, bro. She's after you.

Russell:　I can count on it.

Tosh:　Let's all have a drink.
　　　　　　　*(They gather at the table to toast and
　　　　　　　feast. Grandfather and Chieko float
　　　　　　　off stage, singing.)*

Grandfather:　Moon is rising
　　　over smoking coals of Bon fires.

Chieko:　Soon the night will hear
　　　the songs of lovers meeting.

GLOSSARY

Concentration (Internment) Camps: Ten sites in which Japanese Americans were interned during World War II.

> Manzanar, California
> Tule Lake, California
> Poston, Arizona
> Gila River, Arizona
> Minidoka, Idaho
> Heart Mountain, Wyoming
> Granada, Colorado
> Topaz, Utah
> Rohwer, Arkansas
> Jerome, Arkansas

Total capacity of the ten camps: 120,000 people. Each site was isolated in deserts or swampy delta areas, with severe weather conditions, undeveloped land and soil unsuitable for cultivation.

> "The mosquitos at Rohwer were the worst. Bigger than your baby fist. They'd get through our nets and we could hear them buzzsawing in our ear . . . you were one big mosquito welt. Yea, they loved your soft baby skin for dessert . . ." *(My cousin, John)*

Issei: Generation of Japanese who emigrated to the United States, referred to as the First Generation.

Nisei: First generation of Japanese Americans born in the United States, but referred to as the Second Generation.

Sansei: Third Generation Japanese Americans.

Yonsei: Fourth Generation Japanese Americans.

Bon Festival: In Japan, *Bon* is observed in mid-August to commemorate the spirits of the dead. It is also called the Festival of Lanterns (fires and lanterns are lit to guide the souls to their homes).

Many Japanese American communities celebrate *Bon* during the summer months with songs and dances passed from generation to generation. Originally a somber and melancholy Buddhist ceremony with chants, prayers and dance in a mass for the spirits of the dead, in contemporary times *Bon* has become an occasion for festivity and celebration, the coming together of families and community.

"Tsuki ga, deta deta . . .": Lyrics from "Tanko Bushi" or "The Coal Miner's Song from Kyushu," a folk song and dance popular also in the Japanese American communities for its simplicity of movements which depict the work of coalminers digging for coal and pushing their carts. Sung and danced by celebrants at festivals and banquets.

"Shina no yoru . . .": Lyrics from "China Nights" a song popular in the Japanese American communities during the 40's and 50's. Many Nisei heard and learned the song for the first time while interned in the camps. It is said that the Kibei (born in the U.S. but educated in Japan) popularized the song from Japan in America. "China Nights" is a melancholy and nostalgic love song recalling the past.

Namu amida butsu: A Buddhist prayer/chant. Recitation is an act of reverence to the glory of Amida Buddha.

Shakuhachi: Bamboo flute which has a breathy, haunting quality of sound.

Obi: A long, wide, heavy decorative sash tightly encircled several times completing the kimono outfit. It is bound from the bosom to the waist and tied at the back to display the design of the loop and woven tapestry of the obi.
   The obi compels a straight spine posture.

> "I hate wearing the damn thing. You can't even take a deep breath let alone sing! I think the obi was invented by men to confine our steps and constrict our voices . . ." *(Aunt Chiyo)*

SOURCE ACKNOWLEDGMENTS

Some of the works in *Awake in the River* have appeared in *Time to Greeze!*; *Third World Women*; *Bridge Magazine*; *Counterpoint*; *Aion*; *Asian American Heritage*; *Rikka* (". . . I Still Carry It Around," an essay by Hisaye Yamamoto); *Odes to Bill Sorro*; *Mark in Time*; *Ayumi*; and others.

Some of the poems in *Shedding Silence* have appeared in *Amerasia Journal*; *Bamboo Ridge*; *East Wind Magazine*; *Practising Angels Anthology* (Seismograph Press); *Breaking Silence: An Anthology of Asian American Poets* (Greenfield Review); *Fusion* (San Francisco State Journal); *Hawk's Well: A Collection of Japanese American Art and Literature*; and *Contact II*.

ABOUT THE AUTHOR

Janice Mirikitani (1941–2021) is the author of five books of poetry, *Awake in the River* (1978), *Shedding Silence* (1987), *We, the Dangerous* (1995), *Love Works* (2002), and *Out of the Dust* (2014), the coauthor with Cecil Williams of *Beyond the Possible* (2013), and the editor of nine anthologies. In addition to serving as San Francisco's second poet laureate, she was the executive director and cofounder of GLIDE, a nationally recognized center for social justice, for more than five decades. An award-winning artist and activist, she received more than fifty honors, including the Book Award for Lifetime Achievement from the Before Columbus Foundation, the Minerva Award from the Governor and First Lady's Conference on Women and Families, and the Medal of Honor Award from the University of California at San Francisco Chancellor. At the time of her death in 2021, she lived in San Francisco with her husband, the Reverend Cecil Williams, and was still fighting systemic injustices through her work with GLIDE.

CLASSICS OF ASIAN AMERICAN LITERATURE